SESSIONS WITH SAMUEL

Smyth & Helwys Publishing, Inc.
6316 Peake Road
Macon, Georgia 31210-3960
1-800-747-3016
© 2010 by Smyth & Helwys Publishing
All rights reserved.
Printed in the United States of America.

The paper used in this publication meets the minimum
requirements of American National Standard for Information
Sciences—Permanence of Paper for Printed Library Materials.

Library of Congress Cataloging-in-Publication Data

Cartledge, Tony W.

Sessions with Samuel : stories from the edge / by Tony W. Cartledge.
p. cm.
Includes bibliographical references and index.
ISBN 978-1-57312-555-0 (pbk. : alk. paper)
1. Bible stories, English.—O.T. Samuel. I. Title.
BS550.3.C37 2010
222'.4007—dc22

2010008522

Sessions *with*
• • • Samuel

Stories
from the *Edge*

Tony W. Cartledge

SMYTH&HELWYS
PUBLISHING, INCORPORATED · MACON, GEORGIA

Also by Tony W. Cartledge

1 & 2 Samuel (Smyth & Helwys Bible Commentary)

Intrigued, How I Love to Proclaim It: Adventures in Thinking Theologically

Job: Into the Fire, Out of the Ashes (with Jan Cartledge)

Telling Stories: Tall Tales & Deep Truths

A Whole New World: Life After Bethany (with Jan Cartledge)

Acknowledgments

I am grateful to Smyth & Helwys for the opportunity to share my interest in 1 and 2 Samuel with a wider audience than might be expected to read the 747-page tome I wrote for the Smyth & Helwys Bible Commentary series. Readers who find any of the following pages intriguing are invited to dig deeper in the larger volume.

My own love for the Old Testament was inspired mainly by professors John I. Durham, Elmo Scoggin, and the late Ben Philbeck, all of whom suffered through my questions during a few memorable years (1979–1982) at Southeastern Baptist Theological Seminary.

I offer special thanks to my wife, Jan, and son, Samuel, who didn't complain when I took time away for a "writing retreat." Our dog probably complained about missing some walks, but he had to live with it.

I'm also thankful for the daily encouragement of my colleagues at Campbell University Divinity School, and for the ungrudging help of my graduate assistant Jenny Lee, who proofread the manuscript and offered helpful suggestions.

Dedication

For my parents,
William and Hollie Cartledge,
who raised me with the passion of Hannah,
the wisdom of Samuel,
and a love for good stories.

Table of Contents

Preface

Sessions with Samuel draws on stories from the biblical books of
1 and 2 Samuel that may engage the reader in reflecting on the narrative of his or her life. As the believer's essential storybook, the
Bible preserves traditions that are not just memorable, but valuable,
stories that connect across the centuries because they embody gut-level themes common to every age.

The ten sessions of this book reflect a sampling of stories from
the edge. The people of Israel were at a crucial point in their history.
Dangers lurked both without and within. Decisions made—both
collectively and individually—had ramifications for years to come.
Israel's experience during the early Iron Age was in many ways quite
different from life in our technologically advanced world, but the
underlying questions of what it means to be human and in relationship with others—and with God—are questions that endure.
Questions and conflicts faced by Samuel or Saul, Abigail or
Absalom, Doeg or David may inform and challenge our efforts to
grow in both peace and potential.

Each session begins with a guided tour of a given story, the
questions it raises, and possible connections we might find between
the biblical story and our story. Some texts are too long for a full
treatment, but are summarized in order to fill in the larger picture.
Each session concludes with a series of questions or suggestions for
further thought designed to benefit Bible study leaders or individual readers. Reading a story is just the down payment on growth:
profit comes through reflection.

Introducing 1 and 2 Samuel

Canonical Context

The biblical books we call 1 and 2 Samuel are an integral part of what Hebrew tradition refers to as the "Former Prophets" and what modern scholars call the "Deuteronomistic History." Stretching from Joshua through 2 Kings (with the exception of Ruth), these books relate the remembered history of Israelites from their hopeful entry into the promised land as rising conquerors to their doleful exit as Babylonian captives.

The Deuteronomistic History, though composed from a variety of sources, bears the marks of a common editorial hand. The compiler of the ancient traditions probably worked during the exilic period, though he may have built upon an earlier edition dating from the days of King Josiah, who died in 609 BC. The final work was likely publicized sometime after 560 BC (where 2 Kings ends with the release from prison of former king Jehoiachin) and before 539 BC, when Cyrus II of Persia conquered the Babylonians and set in place a new policy allowing exiles to return to their homelands.

The Deuteronomist is so called because he interpreted Israel's history through the lens of a *quid pro quo* theology underlying the book of Deuteronomy, a system of belief that promised blessings to those who obediently kept Israel's covenant with God, and curses to those who did not. Thus, the Deuteronomist worked with a purpose that went beyond a review of notable events in Israel's history, seeking to explain not just *what* had happened, but *why*. Israel found success when the people were obedient to God, but suffered when they turned away. By emphasizing this theme, the Deuteronomist communicated to the exiles an unmistakable understanding of why they had fallen to such a low estate—but also why hope remained for those who put their trust in God.

Reading 1 and 2 Samuel with an awareness of the larger context helps us see how stories ranging from Samuel's birth and Saul's fall to David's rise and Absalom's death were chosen and related for a larger purpose. Even so, each story carries a unique set of potential meanings for the perceptive reader.

Historical Setting

The events described in 1 and 2 Samuel extend for about a century, beginning with the birth of Samuel (probably before 1070 BC) and ending shortly before David's death, often dated around 970 BC. During this period, the area's traditional superpowers were in decline, opening a window of opportunity for new and emerging states in the Middle East. As Egypt roiled with internal dissent and ineffective leadership plagued both Assyria and Babylonia, small states and strong tribal groups expanded their influence in the Levant, the area bordering the eastern shores of the Mediterranean. Israel was among them.

Samuel, often considered Israel's last "judge," thought the tribal elders' desire for a king showed a lack of faith in God as the only monarch they needed. Even so, Samuel became a key player in facilitating the transition from tribal federation to organized nationhood. Israel's political development did not come without competition: the Ammonites and Moabites to the east, Syrians to the north, and Amalekites to the south also sought to grow in influence. The greatest threat to Israel's emerging state, however, came from the west, where the Philistines built a powerful base of five strong city states along the coast and used it as a platform for deep incursions into the fertile valleys claimed by the Israelites. Only under David were the Philistines pushed back into their coastal pentapolis and held at bay.

Theological Significance

As mentioned above, the Deuteronomistic mantra of blessing for obedience and punishment for sin is the dominant theological theme in the books of 1 and 2 Samuel. The bad behavior of Eli's sons earned a bleak future for their descendants. Samuel's hope that his sons might judge after him was dashed on the shores of their greed. Saul's star rose as he followed God's commands relayed through Samuel, and fell when he failed to do so. David prospered as he sought and followed divine guidance, but even Israel's greatest king suffered the consequences of turning to his own way. Through his selection and editing of the stories, the narrator expresses a belief that Israel's precarious position was due in no small part to its people's proclivity for camping on the metaphorical cliff.

The story doesn't end with judgment, however. Grace appears in unexpected places: David commits crimes worthy of death, but he does not die. He remains on the throne, diminished and chastened, but still the recipient of a promise God intends to keep. Trouble comes, but hope remains.

In 1 and 2 Samuel, Israel faces one crisis after another, a people constantly on the edge. Philistines threaten, leaders fail, kingship disappoints. Yet, each crisis is a gateway for learning: the loss and return of the Ark of the Covenant herald a deeper understanding of God, Saul's failures become lessons for David, enemy incursions inspire heroism and courage. Individuals face crises, too: a young David struggles to survive a Philistine giant and a paranoid king, Saul weeps before a witch as his kingdom falls apart, an older David discovers that the enemy he cannot defeat is himself. Through all the trials, however, God waits in the wings, and hope remains.

Desperate Housewives

1 Samuel 1:1–2:11

S e s s i o n

Have you ever wanted something so desperately that you could see it, taste it, feel it—but you couldn't have it? You could imagine it, fantasize about it, make plans for it, but never actually get it? Maybe it's a particular career you have in mind, or a spouse, or house. Maybe it's a deep-set sense of purpose. Others may not know what you've longed for, but you know. If you've known a desperate longing, you can relate to this text.

The story begins like a fairy tale: "There was a certain man" translates the Hebrew equivalent of "Once upon a time, there was a man" (1:1). And there was a man in the story, a man name Elkanah who lived in Ramathaim (a place more commonly called Ramah), but the story is not about him. It is about his two wives, and both of them were desperate women. You'd be desperate, too, if you walked in either of their sandals.

Desperation (1:2-14)

Hannah felt desolate because she had married Elkanah with all the hopes and dreams of youth, but years had passed and she never got pregnant, and because she bore no children, her husband took a second spouse whose name was Peninnah. Elkanah loved Hannah deeply, the story insists, but Israel's societal norms in the eleventh century BC demanded that he beget sons to carry on his name and inherit his property. Perhaps Elkanah felt that he had no choice, and perhaps Hannah understood the cultural logic behind her husband's decision, but even so, it had to hurt. When wife number two began to produce one child after another, Hannah felt pushed to the periphery. Perhaps she suspected that Elkanah found too much enjoyment in the act of procreating with Peninnah, but she preferred not to think about it. Her husband took pains to remind Hannah of his love, but Elkanah's words brought little solace.

Hannah was not the only desperate woman in Elkanah's camp. Peninnah was desperate because her fecundity brought her a secure place in Elkanah's home, but not in his heart: she knew her husband loved Hannah first and best, and her misery made her mean. As people are sometimes wont to do, Peninnah salved her wounded self-esteem by tormenting her rival. Perhaps she hoped to drive Hannah away, or to make Hannah such miserable company that Elkanah would avoid Hannah's tent and spend more time with her.

Tensions between the women were most intense during the holidays, when the family traveled to Shiloh for the annual harvest days of sacrifices and feasting, a time when the extended family camped and ate together and it was harder for Hannah to avoid Peninnah's harassment.

Feast days were ordinarily times of joy: eating meat was a rare and celebratory occurrence, and wine flowed freely during the festival, but Hannah could not celebrate. When Elkanah carved the roast, the narrator tells us, he gave Hannah a healthy portion (perhaps even a "double portion"; the text is obscure). Even so, the meat on Hannah's plate could not compare with the piled up platter required to feed Peninnah and her brood. Faced with the haunting reminder of her childlessness—and sitting before her taunting adversary—Hannah could not eat.

Hannah's grief was compounded by her well-meaning but obtuse husband's solicitations: "Hannah, why do you weep? Why do you not eat? Why is your heart sad? Am I not more to you than ten sons?" (v. 8 [all citations, unless otherwise noted, are from the NRSV]).

Some questions don't bear answering, and Elkanah had just asked three of them. The narrator piles up adjectives to portray Hannah's pitiable state: she was provoked and grieved (v. 6), sad in heart (v. 7), afflicted (v. 11), and sorrowful in spirit (v. 15). Driven to distraction by Peninnah's persistent picking, Hannah was at her wit's end. She couldn't stay at the table. She was ready to do something desperate.

That something was a tearful flight to the temple, where she made a vow.

A vow is serious business. It is serious business in our own culture, where we think of it as an unconditional promise, and it was serious business in Hannah's world, where it meant precisely the opposite. In the ancient Near East, both in Hebrew life and in surrounding cultures, vows also involved promises, but they were always conditional. In making a vow, an ancient postulant would place a request before whatever god he or she happened to believe in, and promise something in return if the prayer was answered.

Thus, Hannah's blubbering prayer came out like this: "O LORD of hosts, if only you will look on the misery of your servant, and remember me, and not forget your servant, but will give to your servant a male child, then I will set him before you as a nazirite until the day of his death. He shall drink neither wine nor intoxicants, and no razor shall touch his head" (v. 11).

Notice how Hannah accentuates not only her personal misery, but also her position as a devoted servant of Yahweh (God's name as revealed in the Old Testament, most commonly represented by LORD in small capital letters). What she asks for is a boy child. What she promises in return—the most precious thing she could imagine and perhaps the only worthy exchange—is that same boy.

We should point out that the NRSV includes phrases here that are not in the standard Hebrew text (the Masoretic Text, or MT), but that do appear in an early Greek translation (the Septuagint, or LXX) and in one of the Dead Sea Scrolls (4QSam^a). The added phrases, which may preserve an older Hebrew version, indicate that Hannah promised not only that she would return her hoped-for son to live before Yahweh at the Shiloh temple, but that he would live as a Nazirite, a person whose devotion to God would be marked by abstinence from alcohol and razors alike.

Ironically, when the old priest Eli overheard Hannah's sobbing, stumbling prayer, he mistook her agony for inebriation, thinking she had been feasting too long and drinking too much. "How long will you make a drunken spectacle of yourself?" he croaked. "Put away your wine" (v. 14).

Inspiration (1:15–2:11)

Perhaps Eli hoped his caustic remark would send Hannah packing, but her persistence was as strong as her grief. She spoke politely but plainly to Eli, insisting that she was not drunk on wine, but on sorrow (vv. 15-16). Perhaps she explained to Eli the context and content of her desperate prayer. In any case, he changed his tune and sought to console the troubled woman. Eli did not feel confident enough to make promises on God's behalf, but he made a wish.

Speaking carefully, he said, "Go in peace, and may the God of Israel grant you what you have asked of him" (v. 17, my translation).

Hannah received Eli's blessing, ambiguous though it was, as an encouraging assurance that God had heard her prayer. For the first time in many years, perhaps, Hannah dared to think that God might reverse her infertility. High on hope, she returned to the camp with a lighter step and a happier mood. She ate from her plate and adorned her face with a smile. When they got home, she slept with her husband.

And she conceived, because "the LORD remembered her" (v. 19).

The child was a boy, and she named him Samuel, which means "heard of God." "I have asked him of the LORD," she said (v. 20), and the Lord had heard.

Hannah was now a different woman. The cultural shame of a childless woman had come to an end. As hard as it might have been, she fulfilled her promise to God: after the boy was weaned (which could have been as long as three years), and with Elkanah's support, she took Samuel to the temple in Shiloh. There she and Elkanah offered impressive sacrifices, including a valuable three-year-old bull, in addition to leaving Samuel to serve as an apprentice to Eli.

In the act of leaving Samuel behind, Hannah explained her actions with a rather elaborate Hebrew pun that is lost on English readers. The word *sha'al*, in the basic qal stem, means "ask." In the causative hiphil stem it means "lent." In the niphal stem it means either "asked" or "lent." Hannah uses all three forms of the word in vv. 27-28. It is interesting that she does not use the word "give," which she had used in making the vow (v. 11). Rather, he would be "lent" to the Lord. The choice of words probably indicates no diminishment of Hannah's deed, however: she could give him to Yahweh's service, but Samuel would never stop being her child. Hannah remained in touch with Samuel (2:19 says she would take him "a little robe" each year when they went up for the sacrifices), but Samuel remained in Shiloh.

Hannah's shift from desperate grief to overwhelming exultation was remembered in a song. It would have been tempting to gloat in Peninnah's presence, but Hannah chose instead, the narrator tells us, to praise the God who blessed her with a child. We must acknowledge that the "Song of Hannah" in 2:1-10 is a bit problematic. It is appropriately shaped as a hymn of praise, but in some aspects it seems more fitting for a victorious army than a vindicated mother: v. 4 declares, for example, "The bows of the mighty are broken, but the feeble gird on strength."

Other couplets are more appropriate to Hannah's situation: "The barren has borne seven, but she who has many children is forlorn" (v. 5a). Hannah actually bore six children, according to 2:21, which implies she bore three sons and two daughters in addition to Samuel. The number seven, however, indicates fullness or completion in Hebrew thought, and would have been appropriate, especially in poetry.

The heart of the song is the common theme that Yahweh can make the strong weak and the weak strong:

"The LORD makes poor and makes rich;
    he brings low, he also exalts.
He raises up the poor from the dust;
    he lifts the needy from the ash heap,
    to make them sit with princes
    and inherit a seat of honor. (2:7-8a)

The hymn closes with an obvious anachronism, calling for God to bless the anointed king (v. 10), when Israel's first king was actually chosen and anointed many years later—by Hannah's son Samuel.

Inconsistencies aside, the hymn serves its intended purpose, reflecting the joy of a desperate woman who turned to God, saw all her dreams come true, and gained satisfaction over her adversary.

Consideration

What shall we do with this story about Hannah, one of the great heroes of the faith? Does her experience promise that God will answer all our prayers in the way we like, or is something deeper at work?

It is important to note that, while Hannah truly exulted in the birth of her hoped-for son, she found peace at the moment she made her vow and turned the matter over to God. In that act, Hannah recognized that she had done all she could do. She came to an understanding with God and surrendered her problems to the divine will. If God granted her a son, she would return the child to God and be satisfied to visit him in his new home. If God did not grant her prayer, then she would accept this fact with the peace of knowing that she had done all she could.

It is a hard fact of life that prayers aren't always answered in the way we want. When 1 and 2 Samuel was first put together with other parts of the Deuteronomistic History, its intended audience was Israel in exile, a people who had lost their homeland and longed to return, a people desperately in need of hope. There are other kinds of exile. We may have deep longings for a mate, for a child, for a job, for a sense of meaning that seems to elude our best efforts.

What do we do with our desperation? Peninnah felt unloved and resorted to bitterness, seeking to repair her wounded self-esteem by tearing down someone else's. If Peninnah ever found peace, we do not read of it.

Hannah wallowed in her misery for years, but ultimately found both peace and hope when she took her emptiness to God and left it there. The birth of Samuel was a bonus, but no longer essential for Hannah to experience fullness of life. Hannah learned that hope and peace grow from acknowledging our limits and trusting to God what we cannot do for ourselves. Some burdens cannot be borne without serious detriment to our health and well-being. We can, however, give them to God.

Hannah's search for significance is central to the story, but not its only lesson. The theme of generosity is also present. While Peninnah lacks a generous spirit, Elkanah is portrayed as a man who gives not only to his family, but to God. When Hannah returns Samuel to Shiloh, she goes beyond her original promise and adds a significant quantity of sacrifices. Generosity grows from an acknowledgment that all blessings come from God and that we are stewards of God's gifts, called to use them in a way that honors God and furthers God's work in the world.

1. Have you ever known someone like Peninnah who sought to build his or her self-esteem by tearing down other people? Has that someone ever been you? Is this appropriate behavior for Christ-followers?

_____

_____

_____

_____

_____

2. Try to imagine yourself in Hannah's place, cherishing a longed-awaited child for a short time, then surrendering the child to God. Although we generally keep our children at home for much longer, is there some commonality between what Hannah did and the challenge we face to raise our children, teach them to love God, equip them for life, and then give them up?

_____

_____

_____

_____

_____

3. What would you consider to be God's greatest blessings to you? Do you also sense empty spots in your life? Can you trust God with your lack as well as your abundance?

_____

_____

_____

_____

_____

4. Can you name things you prayed for but never received? Has this negatively impacted your faith, or have you learned to find peace in the particular circumstances of your life?

_____

_____

_____

_____

_____

5. If you have children at home, do you ever temporarily entrust your children to other people? Is it hard to leave them under the guidance of a coach, a teacher, a youth leader? Can you imagine giving up your child permanently, even to God?

_____

_____

_____

_____

_____

6. As a practical application, how would you react if one of your children told you he or she felt God's call to work in a land where missionaries are unwelcome and Christians are persecuted? What if he or she felt called to serve in the military? Could you surrender your child to God's care and live in peace?

_____

_____

_____

_____

_____

7. Hannah learned to live in hope and was actively engaged in bringing her hopes to fruition. In October 2009, just nine months after his inauguration as president of the United States, Barack Obama was awarded the Nobel Peace Prize. Surprised by the honor, Obama noted that sometimes the prize is given to boost momentum for a cause, not just to reward accomplishment. Apparently, the Nobel committee believed the young president's active promotion of hope for a more peaceful world was worthy of recognition. In stating his acceptance, Obama called for "a new era of engagement in which all nations must take responsibility for the world we seek." What do you hope for? What are you doing to take responsibility for your hopes?

_____

_____

_____

_____

_____

God in a Box

1 Samuel 4:1b–7:1

Have you ever tried to manipulate God? Few would admit it, but our prayers often betray an attempt to cite our interpretation of biblical promises and then expect God to fulfill them. We are not the first: there may be no better example of putting God in a box than Israel's attempt to use the Ark of the Covenant as a weapon against the Philistines.

The setting is the mid-eleventh century BC, a time when the tribes of Israelites lived as a loose federation and tribal elders made decisions. When enemies threatened, farmers and shepherds were pressed into duty as an informal army that rarely fared well against the seasoned and well-equipped troops of opponents such as the Philistines. The Israelites lacked more than training: they had not yet achieved a proficiency in working with iron, as the Philistines had. The sharper swords, stronger axes, and iron rims for chariot wheels gave the Philistines a clear technological advantage (1 Sam 13:13-22).

A Great Loss (4:1b-22)

The story begins with clear and present danger: the Philistine army mustered near the city of Aphek, near their northern border. Just to the east of modern Tel Aviv, ancient Aphek guarded an important road leading from the coastal plain into the Ephraimite highlands. The Israelites encamped at a place called Ebenezer before venturing into battle, where they lost many troops before retreating in disarray.

Pondering their position, the elders of Israel wondered, "Why has Yahweh put us to rout today before the Philistines?" (v. 3). The elders—and certainly the narrator—interpreted the loss in theological as well as military terms, though they came to different conclusions. The narrator believes Israel is in need of repentance, but the elders decided on a different course. Calling on a "secret weapon," they sought to improve their fortune in the next battle by carrying Israel's most sacred object—the Ark of the Covenant—into battle. The Ark, as reported in the book of Exodus, consisted of a wooden chest plated with gold and covered by a lid (called the "Mercy Seat") that featured two golden cherubim. Ordinarily, the Ark was kept in the most holy place of the temple and thought of as a throne or footstool for the (usually) invisible presence of God: the text describes it here as "the ark of the covenant of the LORD of hosts, who is enthroned on the cherubim" (v. 4).

On occasion—apparently at God's instructions—the Ark was used as a public display and even carried into battle, as against Jericho (Joshua 6). Perhaps the elders felt justified in calling upon the Ark in their time of extremity, believing that Yahweh would give Israel the victory if for no other reason than to keep the holy relic from being captured. It was known that only priests were allowed to deal with the Ark, however, so Eli's sons Hophni and Phinehas were ordered to fetch the sacred symbol from the Shiloh temple and escort it into battle. Given that the two were previously described as "scoundrels" who "had no regard for the LORD" (2:12), the reader has to wonder about the wisdom of the effort.

When the gold-plated Ark was carried into battle, shining like the sun, the Israelites rallied around it and the Philistines quailed, fearing that "gods have come into the camp" (v. 7). Despite their initial trepidation, however, the Philistines convinced themselves to take courage, to "be men and fight" (v. 9). Then, as they fought, troops on both sides discovered that the presence of the Ark did not guarantee the presence or favor of Yahweh. The Philistines won the battle handily. Many Israelites died, and the others fled. The victorious Philistines killed Hophni and Phinehas, captured the Ark, and carried the sacred trophy from the battlefield.

It was customary for ancient armies to plunder their enemies' temples and march back in a victorious parade, carrying idols captured from the opponents. By carrying the Ark into battle, the Israelites delivered their most hallowed treasure to the enemy.

The depth of Israel's loss is recorded in two connected stories. The bearer of bad news was a man from the tribe of Benjamin who ran the twenty miles from Ebenezer to Shiloh with his clothes torn and with dirt on his head. The narrator skillfully raises suspense by having Eli, who is most concerned about the Ark, be the last to know. Though Eli sits anxiously by the gate, he is blind and nearly deaf, so he doesn't notice when the messenger runs through the gate and into town with the tragic news. Tension continues to build, for when the messenger finally reports to Eli, he saves the worst of his four news bulletins until last: "Israel has fled before the Philistines, and there has also been a great slaughter among the troops; your two sons also, Hophni and Phinehas, are dead, and the Ark of God has been captured" (v. 17).

Eli appears unmoved by the news that Israel has fled in battle, that many have been killed, or that his evil sons, Hophni and Phinehas, are among the dead. But, "*When he mentioned the ark of God*," the narrator says, "Eli fell over backward from his seat by the side of the gate, and his neck was broken and he died, for he was an old man, and heavy" (v. 18, my emphasis).

The second story of loss concerns the late Eli's pregnant daughter-in-law, the wife of Phinehas (vv. 19-22). News of the shocking tragedy sends her into labor, which proves difficult and leads to her death. Her last act is to name the child *Ichabod*, saying "The glory has departed from Israel, for the ark of God has been captured" (v. 22). "Ichabod" may mean "No glory," "Alas, the glory!" or "Where is the glory?" In any case, with the loss of the Ark, the people believed that the glory of Israel was gone.

This humbling episode offers a convincing reminder that humans cannot control God any more than they can stop a hurricane. God will be God. A God who cannot act freely but is manipulated by humans is no God at all. Modern believers may try to control God through their particular interpretations of the Bible, or through prayer formulas they believe will obligate God to action. But God is not a genie in a bottle. One secret to growing in our faith is the recognition that we cannot use God, but we find our greatest joy when we allow God to use us.

Eventually, all of us will learn what the Israelites learned in battle that day. Having the paraphernalia of God and having God are not the same thing. Having the title "pastor" or "rabbi" and having God are not the same thing. Being baptized and having God are not the same thing. Those who bring the most goodness to the world and the greatest glory to God are the ones who choose not to possess God, but to be possessed by him.

A Troublesome Visitor (5:1-12)

Yahweh would not allow the Ark to be used like a good-luck charm, but would not desert it, either. A delightful story (for the Hebrews, at least) recounts what happened when the Philistines brought the Ark back to their cities. They came first to Ashdod, where the trophy was set in the temple of Dagon before the image of the god. Dagon was known in the Canaanite pantheon as the father of the more popular Baal Haddu. The Philistines, apparently, had adopted a local god when they entered the land.

The following morning, the image of Dagon was found toppled from its pedestal, face down before the Ark. The Philistine priests propped the idol back up on its pedestal, but on the second morning Dagon was both back on the ground and broken into pieces. The narrator says the head and the hands of Dagon were cut off and lying on the threshold—as if a midnight struggle had taken place and he had tried to get away from the Ark. Dagon was left without a head for thinking or hands for acting (5:1-5).

Don't overlook the narrator's artistic, ironic, and delightfully humorous use of the word "hand." As the hands of the impotent Dagon were cut off, the "hand of Yahweh became heavy" upon the Philistines (5:6-7), terrifying them and striking them with a deathly plague. When the people of Ashdod demanded that the Ark be moved, it was carried to Gath and later to Ekron, two other fortress cities of the Philistines. Trouble followed the Ark, however, for the "hand of the LORD was very heavy" there (5:11), where people also suffered from both plague and panic.

What was this plague? It appears to have been physically manifested in some sort of swellings or "tumors," and an offering later given by the Philistines suggests that it was connected with mice. Commentators often suggest that the outbreak was a form of the bubonic plague, which is spread by rats, but certainty is beyond us. The word translated by the NRSV as "tumors" is the dual form of a word that usually means "hill" or "mound." It could be used for "hips," and the LXX translation says God smote them "on the buttocks." It seems that the narrator enjoyed telling this part of the story, and the medical diagnosis isn't as important as the comedic image of the powerful Philistines being smitten on their behinds. When the scribal Masoretes added vowels to the consonantal text many years later, they gave to the word the vowels for *tehorim*, which means "hemorrhoids." The intended scenario may be that the tumors typically afflicted the rectal area (Robert Alter, *The David Story: Translation with Commentary of 1 and 2 Samuel* [W. W. Norton, 1999] 28–29).

The refusal of Yahweh to save Israel by means of a magic talisman, the silent and hidden encounter between the Ark and Dagon, and the following plagues against the Philistines served to show both present participants and later readers that Yahweh alone is God and will not be controlled by others. The story clearly questions the efforts of religious people to control God, and the validity of any "gods" that have to be propped up when they fall (compare Isa 44:9-20).

There are many such gods. People who would never bow before a graven image may fall prey to the worship of materialism, to the acquisition of things or the accumulation of wealth. Some worship career gods, while others give themselves to leisure. To support opulent lifestyles, we put ourselves under great stress, and to deal with our stress we take longer and more frequent vacations. These, of course, require more money, which puts us under greater stress, which makes us want to get away even more. When our gods fall down, we keep propping them back up.

If we want God's strong hand to comfort us when we are in darkness, to guide us as we walk life's journey, and to lift us up to a higher plane when this world's walk is over, we will want to live without any other gods between us.

A Fearsome Presence (6:1–7:1)

After seven months of misery, the "lords of the Philistines" recognized that the Ark was a danger in their midst. They took counsel with their religious advisors regarding the protocol for returning a god to its proper place, and then set it on a new cart drawn by two nursing cows, accompanied by five golden mice and five golden "tumors" as guilt offerings to Yahweh. The offerings also served as a form of sympathetic magic: the Philistines hoped that by sending golden symbols of their plagues back with the Ark, the curses of mice and disease would depart from their land.

The use of a new cart suggests a sacred purpose, and the employment of two nursing cows seems to have been a sort of divination, testing to see if a deity really was directing the Ark ("milch cow" is not just an archaic holdover from the KJV, but a technical term for a cow who is still nursing her calf). Two cows who were both unaccustomed to pulling a cart and taken from their nursing calves would be most unlikely to leave their stalls and make a bee-line for Israel. That is exactly what happened, however, and it would have been interpreted as a clear sign that a divine power directed the cows to act against their nature.

The narrator seems to have found added humor in the image of the Philistine lords jogging along the nearby hillsides to see where the Ark would go, and what they saw is that the cows came to a halt in a grain field near Beth-shemesh, where a harvest was underway. The Israelites first responded as one might expect: they rejoiced that the Ark had come home and offered sacrifices to Yahweh, using wood from the cart as fuel (since it was clearly too holy to be put to any other purpose) and offering the two cows as burnt offerings.

Not all the Israelites rejoiced, however. In a difficult passage, the text says God struck down 50,070 of the men of Beth-shemesh. This must reflect an error that has crept into the text, for the entire village of Beth-shemesh—much less any single family or clan in the area—would not have counted anywhere near 50,000 inhabitants. Text critics often emend the number to 70, but why would Yahweh strike down even that many? The ancient Greek translation called the Septuagint identifies the offenders as "the sons of Jeconiah," which may reflect a corruption of "sons of the priests." Beth-shemesh was a levitical city that should have had priests on hand, but it appears that the celebratory handling of the Ark and the offering of sacrifices was carried out by people who were not priests, which may be the source of offense.

The story lacks the detail we would like: Were the men struck by lightning? Did they fall as quickly as the unfortunate Uzzah, whose offense in 2 Samuel 6:6-7 was simply touching the Ark in an effort to steady it? Did they catch the plague from handling the Ark, and die slowly? We don't know, but the implication is that the deaths took place in short order, leading the people to draw a clear connection between the men's lack of respect for the Ark of God and their untimely deaths.

The frightened people of Beth-shemesh, as taken aback as the Philistines, were afraid to keep the Ark in their midst. Thus, they persuaded the inhabitants of Kiriath-jearim, about 15 miles to the northeast, to take custody of the Ark. We know little about that city except that it was formerly called Kiriath-baal, which may suggest that it had served as a sanctuary city in pre-Israelite times. Israel's holiest treasure, potentially a key source of inspiration in times of need, remained in cultic quarantine for the next 20 years. Only David would dare to take it up again.

Sadly, this chapter in the history of the Ark concludes with the people of Beth-shemesh doing precisely what the Philistines had done: looking for a way to be rid of a troublesome God. They were not the last to do so, for we remain inclined to worship God when things are going well, but push away when God does not meet our expectations. We prefer the idea of a tame God who answers our prayers and does our bidding, and are less comfortable with the notion of a deity who will not be trifled with, a God who does not live in a box.

1. Have you ever been disappointed because you had certain expectations of God that were not met?

_____

_____

_____

_____

_____

2. Prosperity preachers promote a gospel of "name it and claim it," as if God exists to do our bidding. The idea is quite popular. When Bruce Wilkinson wrote a guide to answered prayer called *The Prayer of Jabez*, it sold enough books to spark a cottage industry. The book is based on 1 Chronicles 4:10: "Jabez called on the God of Israel, saying, 'Oh that you would bless me and enlarge my border, and that your hand might be with me, and that you would keep me from hurt and harm!' And God granted what he asked." Does the biblical account of one man's answered prayer guarantee that others will have the same experience—or that they should try?

_____

_____

_____

_____

_____

God in a Box

3. We tell children that they can have Jesus in their hearts. Adults are more likely to speak of having God in their lives. Is there a difference between "having God" and allowing God to have us?

_____

_____

_____

_____

_____

4. If we give anything in our life a higher priority than serving God, we have effectively erected an idol or false god. Can you think of things, people, or aspirations that you have put before God in your life?

_____

_____

_____

_____

_____

5. Regarding the previous question, have there been ways in which those gods fell and let you down? In what ways have you sought to prop them up?

_____

_____

_____

_____

_____

6. The people of Israel, in multiple ways, misused or showed disrespect to the Ark of the Covenant, the sacred symbol of God's presence. Can you think of ways in which contemporary people trifle with God and disdain what is sacred?

_____

_____

_____

_____

_____

There Goes the Judge

A shaggy-haired man stands quietly on the corner. He holds a hand-lettered sign as weathered and worn as his clothes. The sign says, "REPENT!"

A fervent evangelist warms to the task on the first night of his tent revival. The motley congregation, some of whom came for the free Krispy Kreme doughnuts and coffee, offered few encouraging "Amens." Charging out of the pulpit and onto the sawdust floor, the red-faced preacher shouts, "You people need to repent!"

A youth leader counsels a sobbing teenager who knows that some of her life choices have fallen short of her aspirations. At a loss for what to do, he says, "We all make mistakes, but if you repent of your sins, God will forgive."

What do we mean by this word "repent"? When is repentance appropriate, and what does it accomplish? When the people of Israel found themselves swamped by fear and intimidated by the Philistines, the prophet Samuel led them to a deeper understanding of what it means both to repent and to remember.

What It Means to Repent (7:2-6)

The people of Israel—at least those located in the central hill country, where the early narratives of 1 Samuel are located—lived on the ragged edge. The last we heard of them, the Philistines had defeated them and captured the sacred Ark of the Covenant. The Ark had wreaked havoc among the Philistines, however, so they loaded it on a cart pointed toward Israelite territory. The Israelite folk of Beth-shemesh welcomed the Ark at first, but some members of the community failed to respect the Ark and they experienced a calamitous wreaking of their own, resulting in many deaths. Fearful of

God's presence with the Ark, the people of Beth-shemesh palmed it off on the inhabitants of Kiriath-jearim, a Gibeonite town some distance away.

A transitional verse notes that the Ark remained in Kiriath-jearim for twenty years (v. 2). This indicates that some time had passed, though not necessarily the full twenty years: we don't hear of the Ark again until 2 Samuel 6, when David brings it to Jerusalem.

With the departure of the Ark, Samuel returns to the stage. The last mention of Samuel described him as a young prophet from Shiloh whose reputation stretched from Dan to Beersheba, the traditional northern and southern extremities of Israel (3:19-21). Samuel never appears during the Ark interlude, however, when the invading Philistines probably destroyed Shiloh.

Now Samuel reemerges as a sure and certain spiritual leader in the mold of Israel's pre-monarchic judges. Samuel, indeed, may be seen as the last of the judges, and the remainder of the chapter fits the classic pattern of stories from the book of Judges. The typical form of the "Judges cycle" finds the people of Israel falling into apostasy, which earns divine punishment in the form of an oppressive enemy. When the people cry to God for deliverance, Yahweh raises up a spirit-inspired leader who sparks a defeat of the enemy and then "judges" the people for a certain number of years, usually twenty or forty (examples include Othniel, Judg 3:7-11; Ehud, Judg 3:12-30; and Deborah, Judg 4:1-23, among others). Inevitably the people fall away again, and the cycle starts anew.

Israel's sending of the Ark to Kiriath-jearim serves as a fitting reminder that the people had turned away from Yahweh, so it is not surprising that they experienced oppression from the ever-encroaching Philistines. In the pattern of judge narratives in which the people "cried out to Yahweh" (Judg 3:9; 3:15; 4:3), the Israelites "lamented after Yahweh." The narrator emphasizes the point with a nice play on words: while the Ark of Yahweh remained in the "house of Abinidab" (v. 1), the "house of Israel" lamented after Yahweh (v. 2).

Samuel sought to direct the mourners' spiritual sorrow to more productive ends by promising deliverance if the people would truly repent: "If you are returning to the LORD with all your heart, then put away the foreign gods and the Astartes from among you. Direct your heart to the LORD, and serve him only, and he will deliver you out of the hand of the Philistines" (v. 3).

Samuel's message offers helpful clues to understanding the nature of real repentance. First of all, repentance involves much more than just being sorry for one's sins: "mourning after Yahweh" is only the beginning. The pain we interpret as sorrow for our sins may also reflect the shame of getting caught or the consequences of our actions. As a result, we need to distinguish between feeling remorse for doing wrong and recognizing the pain our wrongdoing has caused.

Samuel's instructions to the Israelites did not focus on the aftermath of their spiritual apostasy, but on its roots: the people had turned away from Yahweh and put their trust in other gods. The Hebrew word we often translate as "repent" is the word "*shub*," which literally means to turn around and return. This is the word Samuel uses in the preface to his remarks, literally, "If with your whole hearts you are returning to Yahweh . . . ." Turning partway around is not repentance: it can't be a half-hearted effort. Wholehearted repentance means turning away from false gods—all of them. We can't turn away from one illicit object of devotion and hold on to the rest. Either we come back to God or we don't.

The temptation to "go after other gods" plagued Israel throughout its existence. To understand this, we must realize that every known culture of the ancient Near East—with Israel at its best a lone exception—was polytheistic. Each tribal or ethnic group might have its favorite gods, but they all believed in multiple deities. The appeal of polytheism, in part, is that there was a god for every need. Since the greatest needs in a pastoral and agrarian society relate to fertility for flocks and fields, the most popular gods were those thought to control the weather and conception.

Among the Canaanites—and Israel always lived among the Canaanites—the foremost gods were various manifestations of Baal and his consort, Astarte. The Hebrew word *ba'al*, common to other Northwest Semitic languages, can be used in human relations to mean "master," "lord," or even "husband." With regard to the gods, it was used as an honorific title, usually for the god Baal Haddu (Hadad), the storm god who was thought to control the weather. When survival depends on timely rains for the grain, it's no wonder that a weather god would be at the top of the list. Images of Baal often portrayed him with an upraised hand bearing a lightning bolt.

Astarte, worshiped alone or in concert with Baal, was an astral deity worshiped in Babylonia as "Ishtar" and in the Levant as "Astarte" (the Greek form of the word), though several spelling variations exist. Astarte is sometimes confused with Asherah, who is probably a separate goddess, though their names occasionally appear interchangeable. As a sign of disrespect, some Hebrew writers vocalized Astarte as "*Ashtoreth*," using the vowels of the word *bosheth*, which means "shame" (the plural, used in 2 Sam 7:3-4, is *Ashtaroth*).

Astarte was the goddess of fertility, love, and war—a powerful ally for those who believed in her powers. Statuettes of Astarte or other fertility goddesses are often found in the remains of Late Bronze and Iron Age cities in Palestine, and were probably a common element in many Hebrew homes. Sacred poles and trees also served as images of Astarte.

The worship of Baal and Astarte, thought to be lovers, often involved feasts, offerings, and cultic prostitution, ceremonies that would have added to their appeal. At times, the Hebrews—or others who worshiped Yahweh—tried to have it both ways, as suggested by an eighth-century inscription on a fragment of a broken jar found at Kuntillet Ajrud. The inscription speaks of an offering made "to Yahweh of Samaria and his asherah," suggesting a belief that Yahweh also had a consort. But Samuel, according to the story, wanted the people to understand that they could not worship Yahweh as just one more local member of the pantheon: they must worship Yahweh *alone*. "Direct your heart to the LORD, and serve him only," is how the NRSV puts it (v. 3). The word translated "direct," however, indicates more than just pointing one's heart in the right direction. It is the causative form of a root that means "be firm," and thus means something like "to make firm," "to establish," or "to fix." As modern radar equipment can "lock on" to a target, Samuel challenged the Israelites to point their hearts toward Yahweh and get a firm fix that would not turn away.

Such a transformation cannot be in principle alone; it must be put into practice. As a demonstration of their return to Yahweh, the Israelites were to put away their Baals and their Astartes. This may have involved the removal and destruction of images from their homes, but may also have required the dismantling of cultic places used by the community (recall, for example, how Yahweh had instructed Gideon to "pull down the altar of Baal that belongs to your father, and cut down the sacred pole that is beside it," replacing it with an altar to Yahweh; Judg 6:25). Such actions would serve as public declarations of fealty to Yahweh and the rejection of other gods.

The people heeded Samuel's instructions; the text says they "put away the Baals and the Astartes, and they served the LORD only" (v. 4). It is worth noting that Samuel waited until he had seen sufficient evidence of true repentance before calling a public assembly to address the conditional promise he had made in Yahweh's behalf, that if they turned to Yahweh with their whole hearts, "he will deliver you out of the hand of the Philistines."

The assembly was held at Mizpah, the site of a previous cultic observance (Judg 20–21 and at least one later assembly in 1 Sam 10). The location of Mizpah is uncertain, but the word means "watchtower," so we presume it was a high place, yet spacious enough to accommodate a large number of people.

Samuel began the ceremony with an enigmatic ritual that involved drawing water and pouring it out before Yahweh. The ceremony, which does not appear elsewhere in the Bible, may have symbolized ritual cleansing or "pouring oneself out" before God. Robert Alter cites the interpretation of the famous medieval rabbi Rashi, who said, "It can only be a symbol of abnegation, that is, 'Behold we are in your presence like this water spilled forth'" (*The David Story: A Translation with Commentary of 1 and 2 Samuel* [W. W. Norton, 1999] 37). Context also suggests that the water ritual symbolized repentance, for it preceded a time of fasting and a community confession that "We have sinned against the LORD" (v. 6). Afterward, Samuel "judged the people of Israel at Mizpah." Exactly what this involved, we do not know, but the context suggests a sermon rather than a law court.

Why It's Crucial to Remember (7:7-17)

Did Samuel suspect that the Philistines would observe the large assembly—seemingly vulnerable and conveniently gathered on a hilltop—and grasp the opportunity to muster for war? We cannot speak to the extent of Samuel's foresight, but the Philistines—whose threatening presence had probably been the cause of the people's "lamenting after Yahweh"—saw a golden opportunity to eliminate Israel's leadership, take hundreds of captives, and make deeper headway into Israelite lands.

For their part, when the Israelites saw the enemy approaching and perceived their predicament, they "were afraid of the Philistines" (v. 7). Recognizing that their position was untenable and their only hope was in Yahweh, they called on Samuel to plead for divine intervention: "Do not cease to cry out to the LORD our

God for us, and pray that he may save us from the hand of the Philistines" (v. 8). Samuel had promised deliverance (v. 3b); now it was time for him to deliver on the promise.

With apparent confidence, Samuel offered a suckling lamb as a burnt offering. Then, as the offering burned—and as the Philistines drew near to attack—"Samuel cried out to the LORD for Israel, and the LORD answered him" (v. 9).

How did the Lord answer? The narrator says that Yahweh "thundered with a mighty voice that day against the Philistines and threw them into confusion; and they were routed before Israel" (v. 10). The image of God intervening in human affairs through storms is common in the Bible. Hymns declare that God speaks in thunder (1 Sam 2:10; 2 Sam 22:14=Ps 18:13; Pss 29; 81:7), as do poetic declarations from the exile and onward (Isa 29:6; Job 37:4-5; 40:9). Lightning was also thought to be part of Yahweh's arsenal (2 Sam 22:15; 1 Kgs 18:38), as was hail (Josh 10:14) and darkness (Josh 24:7).

However Yahweh's "thundering with a mighty voice" was manifested, it was effectively targeted and sufficiently impressive to terrify the Philistines and throw them into a panic. Though the narrator says "they were routed before Israel," it is clear that Israel was not responsible for the routing. Although the Hebrews "went out of Mizpah and pursued the Philistines, and struck them down as far as beyond Beth-car" (v. 11), there was to be no doubt that the victory was Yahweh's, and not theirs.

Samuel, apparently in the midst of the fray and never one to miss a teaching opportunity, marked the extent of the Philistines' retreat with a standing stone and declared its name to be Ebenezer, saying, "Thus far the LORD has helped us" (v. 12). Ebenezer is a compound word: "*eben*" is the word for "stone," and "*'ezer*" means "help," or "helper." Erecting the memorial stone and naming the place "Stone of Help" put in place a perpetual reminder of Yahweh's deliverance, a device for helping Israel to remember the source of all blessings.

The location of Beth-car is uncertain, and it is unlikely that the Ebenezer of 7:12 is the same spot as the Ebenezer of 4:1, where Israel was routed before the same Philistines. There is little doubt, however, that the narrator wants the reader to see that Israel has come full circle from that point: in turning to Yahweh, the once-ravaged Israelites have become more than conquerors. In the following two verses, the writer declares that the Philistines remained within their borders for the rest of Samuel's days and that Israel regained all the towns "from Ekron to Gath" that the Philistines had captured.

In a historical sense, that claim does not jive with later accounts: Samuel still lived during much of Saul's reign, when the Philistines remained a constant threat and maintained armed garrisons well within Israel's tribal lands (Jonathan attacks one of them in 1 Sam 14). The statement is more rhetorical than historical, however: the narrator's point is that as long as Samuel remained in charge, "judging Israel" as he is said to do in vv. 15-17, the Philistines stayed at bay.

This point makes the elders' call for a king in the next chapter jarring. For all Samuel's provisions for remembrance, the Hebrews exhibited a short memory. Despite the prophet/priest/judge's successful leadership, the people sought to trade Samuel in for what everyone else had: they wanted a king "like the other nations."

Modern readers don't have to look far for lessons in this tale of woe and war, human repentance and divine salvation. Preeminently, the story underscores the constant Deuteronomistic theme that rebellion triggers trouble, while obedience brings blessing. But there are minor themes, too: the text declares the essence of true repentance as a wholehearted return to Yahweh who brooks no rivals, and the importance of remembering both as an act of worship and as an aid to spiritual health.

The Philistines were a persistent threat to Israel in part because their skill in the use of iron gave them a technological advantage, and their higher degree of urban civilization provided an edge in organization over the largely rural Israelites. It is interesting that in contemporary English, the word "Philistine" is used to describe uncivilized, materialistic, or barbarian persons or interests. Today we are not threatened by the iron wheels of Philistine chariots, but by philistine attitudes that elevate commercial interests and boorish behavior over faithful living that gives first place to God. This text offers a clear challenge. How will we respond?

1. Think of times of conviction when you "felt sorry for your sins." Can you distinguish between true sorrow over the sin as an offense to God, and sorrow for the discomfort, pain, or trouble the sin brought you?

_____

_____

_____

_____

_____

2. There was a time when frequent revival services led to regular calls for repentance and perhaps multiple trips down the aisle for public rededication of life. Can you remember times of repentance that turned out to be half-hearted? How long did your renewed commitment last?

_____

_____

_____

_____

_____

3. Psalms 57:7 and 108:1 use the same verb found in 1 Samuel 7:3 to speak of one's heart being fixed on God alone. The NRSV, NIV, and NAS versions all use the translation "My heart is steadfast," but the King James Version's "My heart is fixed, O God" has inspired multiple hymns during the past 200 years. Do you have other translations that translate the phrase differently? What do you think it means to have one's heart fixed on God?

_____

_____

_____

_____

_____

4. What contemporary Philistines—or philistine behaviors—threaten your walk with God?

_____

_____

_____

_____

_____

5. How often have you sung "Come Thou Fount of Every Blessing" without realizing what the line "Here I raise my Ebenezer" meant? In the light of this lesson, does the song have more meaning? An early version of the hymn, written by Robert Robinson in 1758, exhibits a close connection between verse 2 of the hymn and 1 Samuel 7:1-14:

> Sorrowing I shall be in spirit,
> Till released from flesh and sin,
> Yet from what I do inherit,
> Here Thy praises I'll begin;
> Here I raise my Ebenezer;
> Here by Thy great help I've come;
> And I hope, by Thy good pleasure,
> Safely to arrive at home.

A revised version of the hymn more popular in today's hymnbooks also keeps the connection, though there is less emphasis on cleansing from sin and more on having one's heart "sealed" (fixed?) in God:

> Here I raise my Ebenezer;
> Hither by Thy help I've come;
> And I hope, by Thy good pleasure,
> Safely to arrive at home.
> Prone to wander, Lord, I feel it,
> Prone to leave the God I love;
> Here's my heart, O take and seal it;
> Seal it for Thy courts above.

Which version do you prefer? Why?

_____
_____
_____
_____
_____

There Goes the Judge

Here Comes the King

1 Samuel 11:1-15

What does it take to make a good leader? What kind of leadership inspires others to follow? Whether they are particularly intelligent, charismatic, or visionary, one essential characteristic of true leaders is that they are willing to lead from the front rather than push from the rear. King Saul's leadership record, like his mental health, was spotty—but for one shining moment, as related in 1 Samuel 11, he became exactly the leader he was called to be.

Israel's transition from a tribal federation led by the occasional spirit-enthused "judge" to an organized state led by a king was not an easy one, and the subject occupies most of 1 and 2 Samuel. One would think, after Samuel's call to faith and Yahweh's demonstration of power in chapter 7, that Israel would be content to trust God as king, with God's prophet acting as an intermediary.

Good prophets were scarce, however, and Samuel's sons did not follow in his footsteps. Rather, although Samuel installed them as "judges" in Beersheba, they turned out to be untrustworthy men who "took bribes and perverted justice" (8:3). As Samuel grew older and the elders of Israel saw no qualified prophet rising up to replace him, they sought a more dependable system of governance. Still recognizing Samuel as their leader, they presented themselves to him and asked for "a king to govern us, like other nations" (8:5).

Samuel was not pleased, believing that the request constituted a rejection of God as king (and him as prophet). At Yahweh's instructions, however, Samuel agreed to grant them a king, but not before citing all the demands a monarch would make and warning the elders of what they were getting into (8:10-18). Undeterred by the red flags Samuel waved before them, the elders persisted in their request, and Samuel sent them home.

What follows are three distinct stories about how Saul became the first king of Israel. In the first, Saul is introduced as a less-than-competent son of a prosperous shepherd who can't keep track of his father's donkeys and who has to get spiritual advice from a servant. Even so, Samuel secretly fingers him as the future king, quietly anoints him, and directs him to a spiritual awakening among a band of ecstatic prophets (9:1–10:16).

In the second account, Samuel summons the people to gather at Mizpah—the same location of their solemn assembly in chapter 7—for the purpose of publicly naming a king. He then casts lots to determine from which tribe, clan, and family the king will come. After narrowing it down to the tribe of Benjamin and the family of Matri, the lot falls to Saul, the son of Kish. Saul, however, again appears as an unlikely choice: he is hiding in the accumulated baggage of the gathered clans and has to be sought out before Samuel can introduce him to the people (10:17-23). Only when his height is mentioned does Saul appear in a positive light: noting that he is head and shoulders taller than others, Samuel declares, "Do you see the one whom the LORD has chosen? There is no one like him among all the people" (10:24). Once again, however, Samuel puts a damper on Saul's acclaim by making a speech defining the rights and responsibilities of the king, including limitations on his power. Samuel then makes a show of writing the rules on a scroll and "laying it up before the LORD" as a precaution against the new king getting too big for his tunic.

When we come to the third account, however, Saul comes into his own as the man of the hour, a leader who is again declared to be king, but this time by virtue of his own spirit-inspired heroism and leadership ability.

A Star Is Born (11:1-11)

The infamous Philistines were not Israel's only enemies. While the Philistines often threatened Israel from the west, the Ammonites sought to take (or retake) disputed lands east of the Jordan, where the tribes of Reuben and Gad claimed their territory. The NRSV inserts a paragraph between 10:27 and 11:1 that is lacking in the standard Hebrew text (the Masoretic Text, or MT), but present in the major Samuel scroll found among the Dead Sea Scrolls (4QSam^a) and in writings of the early Jewish historian Josephus. The added text provides a bit of background to 11:1, claiming that King Nahash of Ammon had made a practice of gouging out the right eye of every Israelite man east of the Jordan, but that 7,000 men still in possession of both eyes had taken refuge in Jabesh-gilead.

Most translations do not include the disputed passage. One can argue that it provides a helpful introduction to Nahash, who has not previously appeared in the narrative, but as Keith Bodner perceptively notes, "the name Nahash means 'snake,' and usually people that bear such names need no introduction" (*1 Samuel: A Narrative Commentary* [Sheffield Phoenix Press, 2008] 103).

As Nahash leads the Ammonite charge, the reader is reminded of Israel's desire to have a king "like other nations" who would "go out before us and fight our battles" (8:20). Such a king might be helpful in combating adversaries like Nahash, whose campaign to bereave each man of his right eye was a clear attempt to humiliate and control Israelites living in the disputed territory, leaving the men with sufficient vision to farm and pay taxes but without the depth perception needed to fight effectively, throw a spear, or shoot a bow with the right hand.

As Nahash and his army besieged Jabesh-gilead, the men of the city sent representatives seeking to arrange a peaceful surrender. Nahash agreed, but only on the condition that every right eye should be gouged out, a distasteful option that led the elders to reconsider (vv. 1-2). Whether Nahash's demand would apply to the men only (who had sent the negotiating party), or to all inhabitants, is not clear. The NRSV and most modern translations insert the pronoun "I" to indicate that Nahash would do the ocular surgery, but the MT leaves open the possibility that Nahash was requiring the Hebrews to scoop out their own eyes, a most unappetizing prospect.

Unenthused with Nahash's offer, the city's representatives asked for seven days' respite in which they might seek a "deliverer," implying that they would surrender without a fight if no liberator could be found. Nahash's surprise agreement may indicate his supreme confidence that no champion would arise and thus the city's humiliation would be even greater.

Nahash had no way of knowing that Saul was about to become a spirit-filled man.

It is important for the reader to understand that the people of Jabesh-gilead and Saul's hometown of Gibeah shared reputations as shamed cities who also had close blood relations as a result of intertribal warfare described in one of the Bible's ugliest stories, Judges

19–21. That story began with a Levite from the remote hills of Ephraim who went to Bethlehem to retrieve a runaway concubine. On their way home, they spent the night in the home of an old man in Gibeah of Benjamin. During the night, a rowdy bunch sought to show their disrespect for visitors by subjecting the Levite to gang rape. The churl refused to come out, but surrendered his concubine to the mob. The next morning, the woman was found horribly abused and dead on the doorstep. Erupting in righteous (!) anger, the livid Levite cut the woman's corpse into twelve pieces and sent one to each of the twelve tribes as a call to action against the tribe of Benjamin, which allowed such offensive behavior from its members.

The other tribes responded in force, leaving only 600 Benjaminite men alive and probably taking all the women as slaves. When they realized how near the tribe was to extinction, however, the other Israelites sought wives for the remaining Benjaminites, but all had sworn not to let their daughter marry one of them. When they learned that the men of Jabesh-Gilead had not responded to the call to arms, they attacked that city, captured 400 young women of marriageable age, and delivered them to the Benjaminites. Thus, Gibeah of Benjamin and Jabesh-Gilead had close ties, related by blood as well as by shame.

We are not surprised, then, that Saul was enraged when the savior-searchers came to Gibeah (whether they also went to other cities is unclear). Interestingly, though the previous chapter declares that Saul has been chosen as king with a contingent of valiant men at his command, he now appears as an active farmer walking his oxen home after a day of plowing when he observes a commotion in town and hears the news (vv. 4-5). Perhaps this preserves an independent tradition of how Saul became king. It may suggest that the transition to kingship took some time and that Saul had to keep farming until taxes started rolling in. Or it may be the narrator's way of indicating that Saul was off to a less than stellar start, slow to grasp his regnal duties.

But that was about to change. When Saul heard (with his ears) what was happening to the people of Jabesh (and their eyes), "the Spirit of God came upon Saul in power" (v. 6). In one sense, this is a positive reflection of the Spirit's empowerment in the Judges stories, but it may also suggest yet another subtle slap at Saul. As Robert Bergen notes, the narrator's choice of "Spirit of God (Elohim)" rather than the more commonly used "Spirit of Yahweh" functionally "deprives Saul of direct association with Israel's covenant God" (*1, 2 Samuel* [New American Commentary; Nashville: Broadman & Holman, 1996] 136). Four of the judges who preceded Saul—and David after him—were infused by the "Spirit of Yahweh." Although "Spirit of God" clearly refers to the same presence, its use may be semantically significant: the only other person in Genesis–2 Kings to be touched by the "Spirit of God" is the non-Israelite Balaam (Num 24:2), who was hired to put a curse on Israel (in Saul's defense, it should be noted that when the Spirit departs from him in 16:14, it is the "Spirit of Yahweh").

Be that as it may, the newly inspired and enraged Saul cut the oxen he was using into twelve pieces and sent them throughout Israel as a bloody call to arms reminiscent of the earlier story of the Levite. Saul's message, "Whoever does not come out after Saul and Samuel, so shall it be done to his oxen!" (v. 7), was both persuasive and effective. There remains a slight shadow over Saul, however. He is not yet confident enough to demand obedience in his name only, but ties his right of command to the authority of Samuel. And, though the people respond to the challenge, it is not because of Saul but because "the dread of the LORD fell upon the people, and they came as one."

With a surprisingly strong army behind him, Saul demonstrated previously unrecognized military skill and cunning. Mustering east of the Jordan at Bezek (about 10 miles from Jabesh-gilead), he sent word to the city elders that Jabesh would be delivered the next day, "by the time the sun is hot" (v. 9). The delighted officials, in turn, put the Ammonites off guard by sending a delegation to report that the city would surrender the following morning, when "you may do to us whatever seems good to you" (v. 10). The prospect of a boisterous eye-gouging party apparently left the enemy camp relaxed and unaware that danger lurked nearby. Using a favorite Hebrew strategy (Judg 7:16; 9:43; 2 Sam 18:2), Saul divided his army into three parts before surrounding the Ammonite camp during the night and launching a surprise attack at dawn, winning a stunning victory (v. 11).

A King Is Crowned (11:12-15)

Following the victory, Saul was doubtless the recipient of much backslapping and public acclaim, but the reader is reminded that some men of Israel had previously shown disrespect for Saul (10:27). Flush with support for the victorious king, "the people" came to Samuel, apparently seeking to identify and execute as traitors those who had rejected Saul (v. 12). Here we learn for the first time that Samuel was present with the army, and for the first and only time in his life, Saul managed to upstage the old prophet.

Although the people had brought their complaint to Samuel, it is Saul who stepped in with regal charity and declared, "No one shall be put to death this day, for today the LORD has brought deliverance to Israel" (v. 13). In his finest hour, Saul showed grace as well as courage, the kind of leadership that engenders both admiration and loyalty.

The people, apparently, also wanted to renew their support for Saul as king (or possibly, to crown him officially for the first time), a ceremony that would allow even Saul's former detractors to pledge allegiance to the king. Samuel, however, preferred to have the ceremony on his own turf, so he led the people south and then back across the Jordan to Gilgal, where the Israelites had originally commemorated their entrance into the promised land (Josh 4:19-24), and where Samuel made periodic stops on his rounds as judge (1 Sam 7:16).

There the people "made Saul king before the LORD" (v. 15a). To describe their action, the Hebrew text uses the word "king" as a verb: literally, "they kinged him" (as a checkers player might say, "King me!"). Whether the act of "kinging" Saul included another anointing or the investiture of a crown, the text does not say. What it declares is that the people "sacrificed offerings of well-being before the LORD, and there Saul and all the Israelites rejoiced greatly" (v. 15b).

"Offerings of well-being," sometimes translated as "peace offerings," were not burned whole on the altar: the visceral fat and the fat tail of the sheep were burned and a portion of meat was given to the priests, but the people ate most of the carcass. Such offerings were commonly brought during the annual festivals, as reflected in 1 Samuel 1:3-4 where Elkanah offers sacrifices and then distributes portions to his wives. Such offerings, then, were typically the prelude to a party, precisely what is described here: "Saul and all the Israelites rejoiced greatly."

Saul had arrived, and despite the sacral aspects of the ceremony, the narrator keeps Samuel in the background, but he will not stay there. In the following chapter, Samuel steps to the mike and delivers a lengthy speech—complete with thunder and rain as special effects—in which he praises his own leadership and pillories the people for choosing to be ruled by a king. Saul could not win: the people applauded him, and Samuel technically handed over the reins of leadership, but then rained (literally) on the king's parade. The next time they met at Gilgal, Samuel publicly withdrew his prior endorsement and repudiated Saul as king (13:7-15).

A Lesson Is Learned

What shall we do with a story like this? For one thing, we can be reminded of the emotional power of anger. Wrath is too caustic to be a constant companion, but there are times when "righteous anger" is both appropriate and even necessary. Saul grew angry when he learned how the people of Jabesh-gilead, perhaps including relatives, were being abused. Jesus displayed anger when he saw God-fearing people robbed of their place in the temple, and he cleared both money-changers and merchants from the Court of the Gentiles (John 2:13-17).

It is a healthy thing for humans to learn to recognize our anger, name it, and examine it more closely. Are we justified in our outrage? Are we mad because someone has offended us (most commonly), or because we see others mistreated? Is our anger based on personal preferences, or on values of justice that come from God? Anger can be a most destructive emotion, but it can also be a gift of God that empowers us to act on behalf of the poor and oppressed. For Saul, his anger became an open door for the Spirit of God to infuse him with the charisma needed to save his kindred from the Ammonite threat.

Saul's behavior after the battle is equally instructive. In response to those who wanted to execute his detractors, Saul not only showed laudable grace to his opponents, but a willingness to give credit where credit was due. He recognized that the victory was not his own doing and confessed, "today the LORD has brought deliverance to Israel."

Saul would not always live up to the standards set early in his reign, but for one moment in time, at least, he demonstrated a standard to which the wise will aspire.

1. What is most likely to spark your anger?

_____

_____

_____

_____

_____

2. Are you moved to anger by the plight of those who are unjustly treated? If not, why do you think this is so?

_____

_____

_____

_____

_____

3. If you do get riled up over injustice to others, what types of abuse anger you the most?

_____

_____

_____

_____

_____

4. Saul was not just moved to anger, but moved to action. Righteous anger has a purpose. Have you taken actions to assist those whose condition angers you? In what ways?

_____

_____

_____

_____

_____

5. Even though Saul was deeply involved in rescuing the people of Jabesh-gilead, he gave credit for the victory to God. Are you willing to give your time, efforts, or resources to help others, even if you don't get credit for it? Can you name any recent examples?

_____

_____

_____

_____

_____

6. When Saul first learned that some "worthless fellows" had criticized him, the NRSV translates that "he held his peace" (10:27). The phrase literally means "he remained silent," or even "he was deaf (to them)." Later, when others wanted to punish his critics, Saul insisted on being gracious to them. What does this suggest about an appropriate response to those who criticize us?

_____

_____

_____

_____

_____

7. How closely does that ideal match our typical response to criticism?

_____

_____

_____

_____

_____

Hacking Agag
1 Samuel 15:1-35

Every year, especially at the beginning of summer and Christmas holidays, the entertainment industry releases a slew of movies that they hope will become blockbusters. The popularity of action movies that glorify violence is enduring, and horror movies continue to attract viewers with their bloody appeal. When the supernatural intervenes, it's usually bad news, and even heroes may have a dark or conflicted side, bearing more pain than glory.

If you like that sort of movie, you'd love a cinematic depiction of 1 Samuel 15, one of the ugliest and most brutal stories found in Scripture. It is dark and foreboding. It points to a side of God—or at least, to an ancient people's understanding of God—that we don't like to see or hear, because it is so much at odds with God as we know him from the New Testament.

Yet, beneath the troublesome parts lies an important lesson for those who call themselves the people of God. So, while parts of this story could be rated "R" for "Revolting," other parts are rated "PG" for "Pretty Good." A couple of verses are rated "X" for "Xtremely Important," but the overall rating is "G," for "God's word." Like it or not, God speaks to us in this text. It is in our Bible. Our task is to understand it and interpret it responsibly.

A Tale of War and Woe

The opening scene features the prophet Samuel, who was at once the most influential and the most frustrated man in Israel. Samuel was influential because God appointed him as a prophet and gave him the authority to anoint Israel's first king and to tell him what to do by delivering messages from God. Samuel was frustrated because Saul, the man God had told him to anoint, showed good potential but didn't always obey the Lord's commands that Samuel passed on to him.

On this day, Samuel came to Saul with a message that God was ready to settle an old grudge with a troublesome band of bedouins known as the Amalekites. Israel had many enemies, but none were more despised then the Amalekites. The heritage of hatred went back to memories of the exodus period, when the Hebrews made their way from Egypt to Palestine. Marauding bands of Amalekites had made a practice of hitting the caravan at the rear, cutting off the weak and straggling. Israel had to stop traveling in order to wage war against Amalek, and prevailed in a long and bitter battle. Afterward, Moses declared what he believed to be a word from God: "I will utterly blot out the remembrance of Amalek from under heaven" (Exod 17:14).

Moses didn't forget. Years later, as Moses gave his farewell speech, he reminded the Israelites to remember this charge. "Therefore when the LORD your God has given you rest from all your enemies on every hand, in the land that the LORD your God is giving you as an inheritance to possess, you shall blot out the remembrance of Amalek from under heaven; do not forget!" (Deut 25:19).

Remembering this word, perhaps, and noting that Saul had attained a modicum of regional power and raised a standing army, Samuel ordered Saul to fulfill the ancient command to eliminate Amalek from the face of the earth. It was to be a Holy War, Samuel declared, a war whose rules demanded twin policies of "take no prisoners" and "take no plunder." Giving orders in Yahweh's name, Samuel instructed Saul to "go and attack Amalek, and utterly destroy all that they have; do not spare them, but kill both man and woman, child and infant, ox and sheep, camel and donkey" (vv. 1-3).

The campaign would have entailed great risk, because the Amalekite camps were far to the south and east of Israel, even beyond the Philistines' coastal strongholds. Leading his main force so far from Saul's base in central Judea would have left Israel vulnerable to attack from another quarter. Yet, neither Samuel nor Saul showed any hesitation in advancing against Amalek. Their confidence, apparently, derived from the belief that Yahweh had ordained the battle and would fight for them.

Saul set out to do just what Samuel had said, gathering an army of overwhelming size and setting an ambush for the Amalekites.

After sending a quiet order for Kenite people who lived in the same area to evacuate, he and his army set upon the Amalekites across the entire southern frontier of Judah. They won a great victory, but there was a problem. The narrator sadly relates that "Saul and the people spared Agag, and the best of the sheep and of the cattle and of the fatlings, and the lambs, and all that was valuable, and would not utterly destroy them; all that was despised and worthless they utterly destroyed" (v. 9).

Did you catch that? The rules of Holy War required that every thing and every creature be destroyed as an offering to God, with no exceptions. Instead, Saul and the troops not only spared the Amalekite king Agag, perhaps to parade him in humiliation as a war trophy, but they also kept the best of the sheep and cattle, and *all that was valuable.* The only things they destroyed were those things that were "despised and worthless."

In the narrator's mind, Saul and his troops could not have shown a more blatant disregard for the command of God as given by Samuel. A verse that foreshadows the end of the story reveals Yahweh's displeasure: "I regret that I made Saul king, for he has turned back from following me, and has not carried out my commands" (v. 35).

Samuel was so bothered by this that he prayed through the night, but while Samuel grieved, Saul basked in glory for his slam-dunk victory and erected a monument to himself in the southern town of Carmel (v. 12) as he marched to Gilgal for an official celebration. The author portrays Saul as being so dense that he didn't even realize he was in trouble when Samuel came steaming into view. Instead, Saul offered a blessing on Samuel and announced that he had fulfilled the Lord's command (v. 13). Samuel responded with sarcasm: "If you've been so obedient, then what is this bleating of sheep in my ears, and the lowing of cattle that I hear?" (v. 14).

Saul caught the drift of Samuel's sneering remark and quickly pronounced what he thought would be an acceptable excuse: "They have brought them from the Amalekites; for the people spared the best of the sheep and the cattle, to sacrifice to the LORD your God; but the rest we have utterly destroyed" (v. 15).

That, of course, did not speak to the narrator's note that they had kept "all that was valuable," and it's likely that that Samuel's face grew red beneath his beard when he shouted a reminder that Yahweh had sent Saul on a mission with specific orders, and Saul had disobeyed them. No doubt Samuel's voice was at a fever pitch as he concluded, "Why then did you not obey the voice of the LORD? Why did you swoop down on the spoil, and do what was evil in the sight of the LORD?" (v. 19).

Saul's response shows that he still did not understand why Samuel was so unhappy: "I have obeyed the voice of the LORD," he said. "I have gone on the mission on which the LORD sent me, I have brought Agag the king of Amalek, and I have utterly destroyed the Amalekites. But from the spoil the people took sheep and cattle, the best of the things devoted to destruction, to sacrifice to the Lord your God in Gilgal" (vv. 20-21).

Saul's defense accomplished three things. First, he unintentionally admitted that he reinterpreted God's command to suit himself by following the spirit of the law, but not the letter. Secondly, Saul blamed the infraction on his troops ("the people took sheep and cattle . . ."). Finally, Saul claimed that his men had no intention of keeping the valuable goods, but only brought them back so they could sacrifice them to God. In addition, it may be significant that Saul did not speak of Yahweh as "the LORD my God," but "as the LORD your God."

Samuel didn't buy Saul's rationalization. In his mind, the commandment had been clear, and Saul had just as clearly disobeyed it. Like a frustrated parent spelling out the rules for a child, Samuel lambasted Saul with a prophetic poem designed to focus the issue:

> Has the LORD as great delight in burnt offerings and sacrifices,
>> as in obeying the voice of the LORD?
> Surely, to obey is better than sacrifice,
>> and to heed than the fat of rams.
> For rebellion is no less a sin than divination,
>> and stubbornness is like iniquity and idolatry.
> Because you have rejected the word of the LORD,
>> he has also rejected you from being king. (15:22-23)

Here is the heart of the matter. No amount of ritual sacrifice on an exalted altar is as pleasing to God as doing what God says to begin with. Saul began to acknowledge his sin, though he still denied having willfully disobeyed Samuel's command. Saul accepted blame only for being afraid to rein in the looting of his troops: "I feared the people and obeyed their voice" (vv. 24-25). That was the kicker, of course. Samuel tried to drive home the importance of obeying God's command. Instead, Saul followed the will of the people (literally, "I listened to their voice").

Saul's spiritual obtuseness compounded Samuel's grief. Saul apparently thought he could simply ask Samuel's pardon and then they would jointly preside over a worshipful offering of sacrifices as if nothing had happened. Samuel, however, refused to attend any ceremony with Saul, and he insisted that Saul's rejection of Yahweh's command had led Yahweh to reject Saul in return (v. 26).

Only when Samuel turned to leave did Saul come to grips with the seriousness of his situation, with the loss of Samuel's (and God's) sanction. A further mistake morphed into an enduring metaphor of loss: Saul grabbed at Samuel's robe as if to pull him back, and it ripped. Samuel quickly interpreted the act as prophetic: "The LORD has torn the kingdom of Israel from you this very day, and has given it to a neighbor of yours, who is better than you" (v. 28).

Knowing that Saul still had hopes of undoing the doom Samuel had pronounced in Yahweh's name, Samuel insisted that Yahweh, unlike mortals, would not change his mind about such a matter (v. 29). Saul's fate was sealed.

Finally humbled but not yet ready to give up, a fearful Saul acknowledged his failure and begged Samuel to help him save face before Israel (if not before God) by appearing with him at the sacrifice. Samuel, being a mortal, reluctantly did change his mind and agreed to go (vv. 30-31), but Saul may have wished he had not. When Samuel arrived at Gilgal, he insisted on doing what Saul had been unwilling to do. He commanded that King Agag of the Amalekites be brought forward, condemned him to death, then took a sword and "hacked Agag into pieces there in Gilgal before the LORD" (vv. 32-33, NET).

Saul remained on the throne for several more years, but he was a lost man from that time forward. He no longer had God's blessing, and though Samuel grieved over Saul, he parted company with the king and refused to see him again (vv. 34-35). The narrator's last cut was the deepest: "And the LORD was sorry that he had made Saul king over Israel."

A Dark and Troubling Story

Modern believers may find this a hard story to like. For many Christians, the idea of a Holy War sounds barbaric and seems to be in sharp contrast to the ethics taught by Jesus, who told us to love our enemies, not slaughter them. Two things will help us in interpreting this passage. The first is to remember its historical context. Samuel and Saul lived in an ancient and violent culture in which wars were sometimes fought for no reason other than plunder, but were often contended as a means of survival. We may hear and understand Samuel's pronouncement of Holy War, but we cannot use this text to promote war over peace, or to declare that our battleships and jet fighters are the instruments of God. We are acquainted with religious fundamentalists who still cling to aspects of that ancient culture, speaking of war as holy or declaring a *jihad* against perceived enemies in the name of God, but people who have read the New Testament should know there is a better way.

To understand Scripture properly (and this is the second thing), we must use the highest point of revelation as the position from which all other passages are interpreted, and for Christians that means that every passage must be subject to the light of Jesus Christ.

The coming of Christ did not bring the end of violence and death, but it did introduce a remarkable new dynamic: Jesus did not set out to slaughter sinners, but to deal with sin. Somehow, in the mystery of God, the way Jesus chose to do that was by allowing the brutality of this world to rise up and kill *him*. Jesus died a violent, bloody death—for *us*. As Jesus suffered upon the cross and took *our sins* upon himself, he made it clear that power and violence as this world knows them must ultimately fall subject to the law of love.

A Clear and Present Point

Now, none of these inherent problems prevent us from understanding the central point of this story, which is straightforward: to obey is better than sacrifice; the inner reality of an authentic faith is more important than any external rituals we can practice. There is more to pleasing God than going to church. Sometimes, as Kenneth Chafin puts it, "We forget that God has always been more interested in our character than our liturgy and more impressed by our compassion than our doctrine" (*1, 2 Samuel* [The Communicator's Commentary; Word Books, 1989] 129).

We cannot read this story without the voice of Samuel persistently shouting in our ears, reminding us of God's call to obedience, pointing out the ways in which we have substituted occasional ritual for daily obedience, and calling us to repentance and renewal.

We cannot read this story without learning from Saul the painful lesson that sometimes repentance comes too late. It is never too late to be forgiven, but there comes a time when forgiveness is accompanied by loss. God did not stop loving Saul, but he could no longer entrust the kingdom to him. God will never stop loving us, but there may come a time when we realize that, in following our own way, we have passed by our best opportunities for serving Christ and accomplishing his work.

1. The term "Holy War" sounds like an oxymoron. Can a war that slaughters innocents really be holy? There's no doubt that Old Testament writers regarded Holy War as an accepted institution, though Jesus appears to have taken a different view. Modern thinkers often speak of a "just war" that is fought in order to defend or rescue an oppressed people, but always with an eye toward protecting innocent life when possible. Viewing the issue through the lens of Jesus' teaching, do you believe God endorses the concept of "Holy War"?

_____

_____

_____

_____

_____

2. The Hebrew language expresses the idea of "obeying" by using the verb for "hearing." As parents often remind their children, if they hear an instruction, they should obey it. In v. 19, Samuel asks, "Why did you not obey ["listen to"] the voice of the LORD?" In v. 24, Saul confesses, "I feared the people and obeyed ["listened to"] their voice." Few people, whether we recognize it or not, are untouched by peer pressure. We want to be accepted, to have what others have, to do what others do. When peer pressure influences positive behavior, it can be good, but we know that it often promotes more negative or selfish behavior. As you make the decisions that govern your daily life, to whom do you listen? Think of several typical choices you make in a day, and consider to what extent those choices are guided by a desire to be obedient to God.

_____

_____

_____

_____

_____

Hacking Agag

3. Although we typically think of "commandments" as being the province of the Old Testament, Jesus also spoke of commands. In the days before his crucifixion, according to John's Gospel, Jesus left his disciples with clear orders, which he designated as *new*. "I give you a new commandment," he said, "that you love one another. Just as I have loved you, you also should love one another. By this everyone will know that you are my disciples, if you have love for one another" (John 13:34-35). The orders are repeated in John 15:12—"This is my commandment, that you love one another as I have loved you"—and again in John 15:17—"I am giving you these commands so that you may love one another." Put those orders in practical terms: what does it mean to live in obedience to Jesus?

_____

_____

_____

_____

_____

4. Though God is forgiving, as noted above, loss may still accompany forgiveness. We may be forgiven for the infidelity that led to a broken marriage, but the marriage may remain unrepaired. We may be forgiven for the bad decisions that led to a night of drinking and driving and a wreck that took another's life, but that life is not restored. We may be forgiven for resisting God's call to mission involvement until we reach retirement age, but many past opportunities for service are then irretrievably gone. Can you think of specific instances in which choices you made have led to loss that remains despite your later desire for forgiveness?

_____

_____

_____

_____

_____

6

A Fool and His Money

1 Samuel 25:1-42

S e s s i o n

It might be a stretch to say "everybody enjoys a good love story," but even macho men can find something to like in a love story that involves vulgar remarks, elements of violence, and a beautiful woman throwing herself at the hero's feet. We find all of those elements in 1 Samuel 25, one of the lesser-known tales from David's early career. Before we get to the love story, however, it is helpful to step back and take a look at the bigger story.

Samuel had officially handed over the reigns of leadership to Saul in chapter 12, but he did not leave, emerging to castigate Saul in chapters 13 and 15 and supervising Saul's descent into a frenzied spiritual trance in 19:24, even though the narrator said in 15:35 that Samuel did not see Saul again for the rest of his life. Samuel dies in 25:1, but still manages a grudging postmortem appearance in chapter 28.

Saul first appeared in chapter 9 and remains on the scene or in the wings through 1 Samuel 31, where he dies (a different version of the same story appears in 2 Sam 1:1-10). Saul becomes a secondary character after 1 Samuel 16, however, when Samuel anoints David as the future king, and the "Spirit of Yahweh" comes upon David while departing from Saul, who is visited instead by "an evil spirit from Yahweh" (1 Sam 16:13-14).

With the exception of Saul's sad visit with the spirit woman of Endor in 1 Samuel 28 and the account of Saul's death in 1 Samuel 31, David appears in every remaining chapter of 1 and 2 Samuel. His rise to kingship, documented in 1 Samuel 16–2 Samuel 5, contains a number of familiar stories: his arrival in Saul's court as a musical therapist (1 Sam 16:14-13), his daring defeat of the Philistine giant Goliath (1 Samuel 17), his friendship with Saul's son Jonathan and marriage to Saul's daughter Michal (1 Samuel 18–19), and his canny ability to elude the paranoid king's pursuit and his unwillingness to kill Saul when he has the chance (1 Samuel 24, 26).

These latter stories, which have much in common, provide a literary frame for the narrative in 1 Samuel 25. Saul began to turn against David almost as soon as the dashing young soldier started making his mark, because his mark was much bigger than Saul's. The cheering women who came out to greet the returning military champions would shout, "Saul has slain his thousands, and David his ten thousands" (18:7). Such praise does not go over well when the big dog gets the smaller bone.

When Saul recognized David as a threat, he first tried to kill the young soldier himself (18:10-11; 19:9-10), and to put David in such a position that the Philistines would do it (18:17, 21). Failing at those attempts, he gathered 3,000 choice soldiers and pursued David throughout the rugged desert highlands of southern Judea. While near En Gedi, according to chapter 24, Saul went into a cave to relieve himself and happened to choose the very cave in which David and his men were hiding. David quietly cut off a piece of Saul's robe, but refused to kill him. We learn in chapter 26 that while Saul's men encamped on a hill called Hachilah, David and his nephew Abishai sauntered into the royal tent after Yahweh put Saul's soldiers into a deep sleep, and they walked out with the king's spear and personal water jug. Despite Abishai's urging, David again refused to kill his nemesis. In both cases, David appeared to the king, waving the evidence of Saul's close call, and asking why Saul continued to pursue him. In both cases, a crestfallen Saul confessed that David was a better man than he and promised to leave him alone.

Between those two stories, we find the account of David and Nabal—and Nabal's charming wife, Abigail. On many counts, we will discover that Nabal and Saul have much in common.

A Mean and Surly Man (25:2-13)

In the framing stories of 1 Samuel 24 and 26, David steadfastly refuses to kill Saul, whom he addressed as "my father" (24:11). Saul is chastened in both stories, referring to David as "my son" (24:16; 26:17, 21). When David encounters another father figure in chapter 25, he comes much closer to shedding blood. While stories surrounding this text portray David in an overwhelmingly positive fashion, the account of his encounter with Nabal first hints that David has a dark side that will kill for a grudge.

The story begins with the same phrase that begins 1 Samuel: "There was a certain man" (v. 2; cf. 1:1). The roundabout introduction allows the narrator to build an impressive picture of a wealthy and powerful man before revealing his name, which declares him to be a fool.

The man lived in Maon, part of a rough region of southern Judah that was one of David's favorite haunts (23:24-25). The bulk of the man's property, however, was in the vicinity of Carmel, a smaller village a short distance to the north. Both were in the area surrounding the important southern city of Hebron, whose biblical history as a favored dwelling place goes back to Abraham. In a culture where wealth was measured in livestock, the man was very rich, possessing 3,000 sheep and 1,000 goats.

There is more to making a great man than wealth, however, and the narrator notes that the rich man's name was Nabal. Any Hebrew reader would raise an eyebrow, knowing that the word *nabal* means "fool" or "lout," and the same consonants with different vowels can be used to describe a wineskin (the original text was written without vowels). As we will see, both Nabal's foolishness and his affinity for wine play heavily into the story. Nabal's wife, in contrast, is named Abigail, a pleasant moniker that means something like "joy of my father."

In the unlikely event that a reader might miss the significance of the names, the narrator offers a parenthetical aside: "The woman was clever and beautiful, but the man was surly and mean; he was a Calebite" (Hebrew *kalibi*, v. 3). The last remark is open to dual interpretations. The descendants of Caleb had a noble history (Joshua 14) and had become a prominent clan, reminding the reader that Nabal belonged to an influential family. A Hebrew reader, however, might recall that *kalibi* can also mean "like a dog."

The reader who suspects that Nabal and David are likely to butt heads before the story is over will not be disappointed. The situation leading up to the conflict, however, is more ambiguous. David had a lot of mouths to feed—a private army of 600 men and possibly their dependents—and the wilderness provides limited forage for a roving band with no property or steady jobs. If the following account is representative of David's typical behavior, it gives the appearance that he went a step further than relying on freewill donations, and ran a sort of protection racket. Apparently David's men stationed themselves around the flocks or fields of property owners and "defended" them, if only against themselves. They then presented a bill for services rendered.

So it was that David sent a delegation of no less than ten men to Nabal during sheep-shearing time, when the flock was fleeced and Nabal was flush with profit from his wool operations. If David had his way, the sheep wouldn't be the only ones getting fleeced. David's message dripped with politeness that failed to cover a veiled threat: "Peace be to you, and peace be to your house, and peace be to all that you have. I hear that you have shearers; now your shepherds have been with us, and we did them no harm, and they missed nothing, all the time they were in Carmel. Ask your young men, and they will tell you. Therefore let my young men find favor in your sight; for we have come on a feast day. Please give whatever you have at hand to your servants and to your son David" (vv. 6-8).

David's message begins with a threefold *shalom*, a word that means "well-being," and closes with an obsequious *faux*-family reference to "your servants and to your son David" (another reminder of Saul, whom David called "my father" in 24:11). Between the patronizing and deferential remarks, however, is a bald "request" for Nabal to "give whatever you have at hand to your servants and to your son David." Since David had 600 armed men at his disposal, there were sharp teeth within the warm and fuzzy bookends of the message.

However David intended the message, Nabal interpreted it as extortion and replied as befitting his characterization as a mean and surly man. "Who is David?" he asked. Then "Who is the son of Jesse?"—revealing that he knew precisely who David was. Nabal's language echoes that of Saul, who had used "son of Jesse" in a derogatory fashion (1 Sam 20:30-31; 22:7-8, 13). Some have speculated that Nabal was a supporter of Saul, who earlier had erected a monument to himself at Carmel (15:12), the same site where Nabal kept his sheep. Nabal apparently knew that David's companions included "Everyone who was in distress, and everyone who was in debt, and everyone who was discontented . . ." (1 Sam 22:2). Debtors could be forced into slavery, so it is likely that some of David's band were runaways. As a wealthy property owner with servants of his own, Nabal would not have approved.

Implying that David—who had fled from Saul's service—was no better than the rabble in his fighting force, Nabal spat words of rejection: "There are many servants today who are breaking away from their masters. Shall I take my bread and my water and the meat that I have butchered for my shearers, and give it to men who come from I do not know where?" (vv. 10-11).

David responded, when his envoys returned, with an uncharacteristic outburst of his own. The disciplined self-restraint David had shown toward Saul in chapters 24 and 26 was pushed to the background as David ordered his men to strap on their swords and joined them in doing so. The bloody raid David anticipated, however, was fraught with danger—not to David's life, but to his hitherto glowing reputation. David suddenly appears capable of angrily killing fellow countrymen in order to get what he wants. This is the first glimpse we get of David's shadow side, which emerges full blown in the Bathsheba/Uriah affair (2 Samuel 11–12). Nabal is not the only man in danger.

A Beautiful and Charming Woman (25:14-38)

David is saved, however, and not for the first time, by a woman. His wife Michal had engineered a ruse that allowed him to escape from Saul (1 Sam 19); now his rescue comes in the form of another man's wife who reaches out to David and throws her own husband under the bus.

Abigail learned of David's request and Nabal's rude reply from a servant who had overheard the conversation. The servant confirmed the claim of David's men that they had not harmed or humiliated Nabal's shepherds, nor taken anything from them. Using a metaphor that becomes significant in the story, he added, "they were a wall to us both by night and by day, all the while we were with them keeping the sheep" (v. 16). Modern translations tend to gloss over the servant's closing comment about Nabal. The NRSV has the servant saying, "he is so ill-natured that no one can speak to him" (v. 17b); "ill-natured" translates the idiom "son of Belial" or "son of worthlessness." Those are strong words previously used to describe the wicked sons of Eli (2:12) and the scoundrels who had repudiated Saul (10:27)—not the sort of language one would expect a servant to use in speaking to his master's wife. Though he is described as "one of the lads" (the word for "lad" can also mean "servant"), we get the impression that the servant is well known and trusted, confident enough to outline the present danger against Nabal "and all his house," and to address Abigail with the imperative, "Now therefore know this and consider what you should do . . ." (v. 17a).

A Fool and His Money

Abigail, as we've been told, was quick-witted, and indeed she did know what to do. Without waiting (as Nabal had previously made David's messengers wait, v. 9), Abigail raided the larder and cobbled together a sizeable gift of food, including bread, wine, dressed sheep, and even dessert items like raisins and dried fig cakes. She then sent them ahead of her as she went to meet David in a manner reminiscent of Jacob sending advance gifts before his meeting with Esau (Genesis 33). Pointedly, she acted without breathing a word of it to Nabal (vv. 18-19).

The narrator artfully sets up the meeting between Abigail and David as they descend from two adjoining hills. For his part, David is complaining and cursing: "Surely it was in vain that I protected all that this fellow has in the wilderness, so that nothing was missed of all that belonged to him; but he has returned me evil for good. God do so to David and more also, if by morning I leave so much as one male of all who belong to him" (vv. 21-22; note the good/evil theme was also present in 24:17).

Modern translations obscure the earthiness of David's curse in v. 22, though it is accurately preserved in the KJV: "So and more also do God unto the enemies of David, if I leave of all that pertain to him by the morning light any that pisseth against the wall." A unique appendage associated with a Y chromosome allows such activity, so the expression became a euphemism for "male." The indelicate idiom occurs several other times in the Old Testament (1 Kgs 14:10; 16:11; 21:21; 2 Kgs 9:8), always with reference to the extermination of all males in a particular household. In context, the euphemism is particularly apropos, for David and his men had been "a wall" of protection for Nabal. David's ire was fueled by the notion that crabby Nabal was piddling against his wall.

As David descended one hill, wreathed in dark curses, Abigail descended "under cover of the mountain," probably suggesting that she could see David and his men coming in battle array, but they would not have noticed her prior to her surprise arrival, perhaps as they paused to inventory the gifts she had sent ahead. When comely Abigail arrived, she hurriedly dismounted from her donkey and threw herself face down at David's feet as the prelude to an eloquent speech (vv. 26-31) that commentators have noted is the longest bit of discourse attributed to a woman in the entire Bible. As David had instructed his messengers to address Nabal with careful diplomacy, so Abigail skillfully attracted David's attention and curried his favor through an overt show of humility, calling David "my lord" (or "master") eight times and speaking of herself as "your handmaid" (or "servant") six times.

Rare is the man who would be unmoved by a beautiful woman falling at his feet, asking to "speak in his ears," and repeatedly addressing him as master while identifying her lovely self as his handmaid, and David was no exception. Abigail began with a quick two-step, begging David to put the blame on her for Nabal's offense, while making it clear that Nabal deserved full credit. Abigail's speech, in fact, reveals that her sympathies were with David and not with her boorish husband. Like the servant, she referred to Nabal with the word "Belial" as a sign of his base nature (NRSV translates "this ill-natured fellow"), and pleaded with David not to take him seriously (literally, "do not set it to heart"). She then brashly removed any doubt about the significance of Nabal's name: "for like his name, so is he: Fool is his name, and foolishness is with him" (my translation).

Nabal's winsome wife portrayed her husband as an incompetent dolt who couldn't be trusted, so she had to go behind him and clean up his messes. Again, Abigail asked David to put the blame on her, though it is clear that her fault was limited to having failed to see and intercept David's messengers before they reached Nabal.

Abigail further charmed David by wishing a curse upon his enemies in a way that is both skillful and shocking. First, she presumed aloud that her intercession was successful: "since the LORD has restrained you from bloodguilt and from taking vengeance with your own hand . . . ." After such a statement, David could hardly proceed with his planned attack. In near scandalous fashion, Abigail then used her own husband as the object of the curse: "now let your enemies and those who seek to do evil to my lord be like Nabal" (v. 26). Why would she wish that David's enemies be like Nabal, since her husband was happily feasting at the time? Perhaps Abigail had let slip a personal wish for Nabal's demise, or a belief that his doom was sure.

By this point, David should have been fully enraptured, but Abigail's seductive ammunition was not yet spent. Confident that David would now avoid unnecessary bloodshed, she looked into his future and predicted great things for him (vv. 28-31). "The Lord will certainly make my lord a sure house," she said, in a proleptic parallel to 2 Samuel 7, where the prophet Nathan declares Yahweh's promise to give David an everlasting "house," or dynasty. If any should rise up against David, Abigail predicted, it would be to no avail, for David would be "bound up in the bundle of the living under the care of the LORD your God," while those who sought to harm him would be slung away like a stone from the pocket of a sling. It appears that Abigail was quite familiar with David and knew he would find the slingshot metaphor meaningful.

Such lilting words would have been music to David's ears, but Abigail had yet another step for his pedestal: "When the LORD has done to my lord according to all the good that he has spoken concerning you, and has appointed you prince over Israel, my lord shall have no cause of grief, or pangs of conscience, for having shed blood without cause or for having saved himself" (vv. 30-31a). In effect, Abigail predicted that David was destined to become king—so long as he remained guiltless of shedding innocent blood.

David, no doubt, was a goner already, but Abigail had one more card up her sleeve: "And when the LORD has dealt well with my lord, then remember your servant" (v. 31b). Did she deliver that last line with a wink or a coquettish grin? There seems little doubt that Abigail was proposing an alliance with bells in the background.

David's response attempts to be stern but sounds almost giddy. He would indeed have become guilty of innocent blood if Abigail had not interceded, he admitted (vv. 32-34). Thus, he blessed Yahweh, blessed Abigail's good sense, and then blessed Abigail herself for having saved him from grievous error.

Any astute reader can guess by now that there is a love story in the works, but there is a major obstacle to its consummation. That problem is soon resolved, however. Abigal returned home to find Nabal in a drunken stupor, having feasted "like a king," yet another similarity to Saul. Purposefully, she said nothing until the next morning. Then, "when the wine had gone out of him"—or possibly, "as the wine was going out of him" (against a wall?)—Abigail explained how close he had come to being murdered in his own house. Nabal responded to the shock of her news by promptly having a heart attack or a stroke: "his heart died within him; he became like a stone" (v. 37). About ten days later, the narrator says, "the LORD struck Nabal, and he died" (v. 38).

Thus, it appears, David received a just rewarded for withholding vengeance and putting his trust in Yahweh. His opponent was neatly eliminated, and David acquired no guilt in the process.

He would soon acquire Nabal's wife, however.

A More Perfect Union (25:39-42)

After learning that Nabal was dead, David wasted no time in laying claim to Abigail. Instead of proposing in person, though, he sent a message that sounds both presumptive and sexist to modern ears: "David has sent us to you to take you to him as his wife" (v. 40). Presumptive or not, the text leads us to believe that this is precisely what Abigail wanted, and she responded with overt, almost overdone humility. Speaking as if David were present, rather than to the messenger, she declared herself willing to wash the feet of David's servants.

Abigail had no intention of being a foot-washer, however. She hurriedly mounted her donkey and followed the messengers back to David, accompanied by five handmaids. This is the fourth time Abigail is pictured as hurrying in response to David (vv. 18, 23, 34, 42), and her five personal maids are the most ever mentioned in Scripture, a hint at the extent of her wealth.

David's marriage to Abigail was profitable on many fronts. He gained a lovely wife who apparently adored him, access to her considerable wealth, and also kinship ties with the powerful Calebite clan, who controlled the important city of Hebron—the very place where David would first be crowned as king (2 Sam 2:1-4).

The Power of a Name

Names play a significant role in this account, which has many human characters, but only three who are named: Nabal, Abigail, and David. Nabal's name means "fool," and he acted as the prototypical rich fool who also appeared in Jesus' stories (Luke 12:13-21; 16:19-31).

Abigail's name reflects the joy of a father. In such names, the element "my father" had divine overtones. Abigail is presented as a righteous woman who suffered a brutish husband in what was probably an arranged marriage for as long as he lasted, a woman who saved David from himself and ultimately saved Israel by preserving David's reputation, and a woman who exhibited the gift of prophecy in foreseeing David's future.

David's name is also significant. It means "beloved." The reader knows that David is beloved of God, anointed to become the next king, and chosen to serve God in a special way.

Those who bear the name "Christian" have also been given a special name—and the responsibility of living up to it.

1. If you could assign yourself a name based on your character, what would it be?

_____

_____

_____

_____

_____

2. If your spouse or close friends were asked to choose a name for you, would the names be similar to the one you chose?

_____

_____

_____

_____

_____

3. The motif of hurrying is prominent in this account, always with reference to Abigail, who is always doing the proper thing. Do you typically volunteer quickly when a need arises, or do you tend to hold back until begged? Think of some examples.

_____

_____

_____

_____

_____

4. When you see a wrong that needs righting, do you act on it promptly or decide to think about it for a while? Can you name some examples?

_____

_____

_____

_____

_____

5. When cross words or a disagreement come between you and a friend or family member, do you step forward to repair the breach or sit back and wait for others to come to you? What would Abigail do?

_____

_____

_____

_____

_____

6. David was fortunate in that Abigail "staged an intervention" and saved him from committing an egregious error. When have others sought to save you from yourself by pleading with you to be less selfish, spend more time with your family, stop smoking, get more exercise, or the like? How did you respond?

_____

_____

_____

_____

_____

7. Do you know someone now who needs to be saved from harm they are doing to themselves? Can you think of ways you could carefully and tactfully help the person find a better way?

_____

_____

_____

_____

_____

Real Men Do Cry
2 Samuel 1:1-27

What do you do when faced with tragedy? Do you cry out in grief, cringe in denial, act out in anger, resign yourself to misery? We have multiple options when faced with loss, hard times, or other crises. Some responses are healthful; some are not. In 2 Samuel 1, David is confronted with heart-wrenching news that brings personal pain as well as dangerous implications for all of Israel. A look at his response to crisis may prove instructive as we deal with storms of our own.

Death, Grief, and Action (1:1-16)

The shift from 1 Samuel to 2 Samuel begins with a portentous phrase: "After the death of Saul" (reminiscent of "After the death of Moses" in Josh 1:1 and "After the death of Joshua" in Judg 1:1). A major change is about to take place, and the first five chapters of 2 Samuel concern themselves with David's management of the awkward transition from Saul's death on Mount Gilboa to his own ascension to the throne in Jerusalem. Samuel had quietly anointed David to be the next king years before, but there was no guarantee that Saul's former allies would recognize David as the legitimate heir to the throne. David needed to exercise deft leadership and political savvy in order to gain both the kingship and the allegiance of the people he would rule.

A bit of background may be helpful: in the latter part of 1 Samuel, the narrator seeks to describe two consecutive storylines by interlacing accounts of what both David and Saul did in the tumultuous days leading up to this point. After succeeding for at least the third time in eluding Saul's constant efforts to kill him, David apparently decided the easiest way to remain out of reach was to defect (at least outwardly) to the Philistines. So, in a bold and radical move described in 1 Samuel 27, David offered himself as a vassal to Achish, ruler of the Philistine city state of Gath. Achish accepted David's offer and assigned him the southern city of Ziklag.

David then played an artful game of raiding various people groups in the area, leaving no one alive to tell the tale in the towns he conquered. He distributed most of the plunder among the elders of Judah, and then delivered a smaller portion to Achish, pretending that he had gained the goods by raiding his own countrymen (1 Sam 27:8-12). Thus David managed to stay clear of Saul, gain Achish's trust, and build stronger ties with the people of Judah.

With 1 Samuel 28, the narrator focuses on Saul, revealing that the Philistines had mustered their forces for a massive battle near Mount Gilboa, deep in Israelite territory. Facing overwhelming odds and desperate for counsel, Saul persuaded a spirit woman to call up Samuel from the grave, but the cranky post-mortem prophet predicted only that Saul and his sons would join him in Sheol the following day.

Meanwhile, we learn in 1 Samuel 29–30 that Achish had called David and his men to join him in the upcoming battle. This put David in a precarious position, for the last thing he wanted to do was fight against Saul. He was delivered of his predicament by the other Philistine leaders, who did not trust David, and with good reason. Achish sent David home to Ziklag, where he discovered that a roving band of Amalekites had plundered and burned his town. David led his tired troops in pursuit of the Amalekites and succeeding in rescuing all the captive wives and children and recovering the stolen property.

While David fought Amalekites far to the south, the battle heated up on Mount Gilboa. In chapter 31, the narrator switches to the climactic scene of that war, describing Israel's overwhelming defeat. Saul had stationed his fighters on the rugged slopes of the mountain in an attempt to take the Philistine chariots out of play, but they were still overrun by the enemy's superior forces. Saul's sons were killed and Saul was seriously wounded by fire from Philistine archers. Afraid that the Philistines would capture him alive and make sport of him, Saul ordered his armor bearer to end his life, but the soldier refused to strike his king. Thus, the narrator declares, Saul fell upon his own sword and died, and his faithful man-at-arms followed suit (1 Sam 31:5-6).

When the Philistines identified the bodies of Saul and his sons, they cut off Saul's head and sent messengers to all their cities, bearing news of the victory. They fastened the bodies of Saul and his sons to the wall of Beth-shan, an important city near the junction of the Jezreel and Jordan valleys, but a valiant group of men from Jabesh-gilead came by night and surreptitiously recovered the bodies for a decent burial.

With 2 Samuel 1, the spotlight switches back to David and does not depart from him for the remainder of the book. David and his men had been back in Ziklag for two days, the narrator tells us, when they saw a man approaching the camp. With ripped clothing and dirt on his head, it was clear that he bore bad news, but for whom? David was a Hebrew, but in Philistine territory, and the visitor was unknown to him. Thus, when the man fell at David's feet, David asked from where he had come. The man claimed to have "escaped from the camp of Israel," implying that he had fought on Israel's behalf. David feared the worst, his anxiety showing in the command, "How did things go? Tell me!"

The Amalekite proceeded to recount a story of Saul's death (vv. 4-10) that differs significantly from the account in 1 Samuel 31. He mentioned the deaths of Saul and Jonathan only, while 1 Samuel 31 records the deaths of three royal sons. The loyal armor bearer who refused to end Saul's misery is absent from the Amalekite's tale. Whereas the earlier account suggests that Saul fought from the mountain crags where only the Philistine archers could reach him, David's visitor insisted that the Philistine chariots and horsemen had been bearing down on Saul, which suggests a different location.

The Amalekite claimed that he "just happened to be on Mount Gilboa" when he came across a severely wounded Saul who was leaning on his spear for support and in danger of imminent capture. David might have wondered how anyone could "just happen" to be in the middle of a battle zone, but the image of Saul and his spear rang true, and he did not interrupt. David knew from uncomfortable experience that Saul was rarely parted from his spear (1 Sam 13:22; 18:10-11; 19:9-10; 20:3; 22:6; 26:7).

Saul had asked his identity, the young man said, and when Saul learned that he was an Amalekite, he explained the depth of his misery and ordered the man to finish him off. Thus, the man told David, "So I stood over him, and killed him, for I knew that he could not live after he had fallen" (2 Sam 1:10). Then, he said, not wanting Saul's crown and royal armband to become Philistine prizes, he had brought them to David.

Real Men Do Cry

How do we explain the discrepancy in the stories? Some commentators have argued for an awkward conflation of two different sources, but the general consensus among recent scholars is that the text implies the young man was lying. He was, after all, an Amalekite, and thus had questionable motives. It seems likely that the man was scavenging among the corpses on the battlefield when he came across Saul's body before the Philistines did. Rather than trying to give Saul a quick burial, however, he took Saul's royal insignia and brought them to David, hoping for a reward. Suspecting that David may have wanted Saul dead, perhaps he concocted the story about giving Saul the *coup de grace* in hopes of gaining even greater favor.

A few scholars contend that there could be some veracity in both stories, proposing that Saul and his armor bearer had indeed fallen on their swords, and that Saul would have died but was not yet dead when the Amalekite happened upon them, so he asked the foreigner to do what his Israelite soldier was unwilling to do.

Whatever we may surmise today, David had nothing to go on but the young man's story, and he could not deny the presence of Saul's familiar crown and armband. Saul and Jonathan were dead, and for the moment, that was enough to deal with. David tore his clothes, as did those with him (v. 11), then "mourned and wept, and fasted until evening for Saul and for his son Jonathan, and for the army of the LORD and for the house of Israel because they had fallen by the sword" (v. 12).

The depth of David's grief appears to be genuine: a more literal translation is, "they wailed and wept and went without food until evening because of Saul and Jonathan his son, and for the people of Yahweh and for the house of Israel . . . ." David's sorrow was both deep and broad: he cried not only for Saul and Jonathan who had died by the sword, but also for "the people of Yahweh and the house of Israel" who would now be easy prey for the Philistines.

Not until evening did David turn his thoughts back to the man who had reported such ill tidings. Although the man had already identified himself as an Amalekite while relating his story, David returned to the point and bluntly asked the news-bearer from where he had come. Perhaps David's question caused the man to grow edgy, for the Hebrew suggests a halting response: "The son of a man (I am), a sojourner, an Amalekite."

The man's growing danger did not arise from his family background, however, but from his actions: the more important question was, "Were you not afraid to lift your hand to destroy the LORD's anointed?" (v. 14). Without pausing for an answer, David ordered one of his soldiers to strike the Amalekite and kill him (v. 15). For David, the man's guilt was self-evident: the man had confessed to killing Saul; his blood was on his own head (v. 16).

Two interesting things stand out. One is an abundance of irony. Saul lost his kingdom because he was ordered to eradicate all the Amalekites, including the Amalekite king, but did not do so. Israel's king then lost his life after ordering one of the Amalekites he had not slain to kill him. David, who previously showed an ability to eliminate entire villages of Amalekites and leave no one alive, did what Saul was unwilling to do and cut down the one he believed had struck down Saul.

David's execution of the Amalekite had little to do with the man's ethnicity, however. He could have been a Girgashite, a Moabite, or even a Hebrew, for that matter. The man had killed the king, and David had a clear opinion about regicide. Twice David could have killed Saul, but both times he had refused to harm "the LORD's anointed" (1 Sam 24:6-7; 26:9-11). Since David was also anointed in Yahweh's name as the prospective king, one suspects a measure of self-interest in his proclamation of an absolute taboo on harming the Lord's anointed. David's quick work in dispatching the Amalekite emphasized his own innocence in Saul's death, and his displeasure with it—something that becomes a common theme in the next few chapters.

Loss and Lamentation (1:17-27)

David's manifestation of grief for the loss of Saul and Jonathan was no act for the cameras, although it would have been astute for him to mourn the king's death whether he was truly touched or not. In the narrator's mind, at least, David's distress was genuine, born of deep love and friendship with Jonathan and of constant respect for King Saul.

Beyond the initial display of ripping his robe, weeping, and fasting, David composed a personal lament and then commanded that it be taught to the people of Judah (v. 18). The Hebrew text is difficult; a literal reading is "he said to teach the sons of Judah the bow." It is clear that David's command had nothing to do with archery, because the next line declared, "behold, it is written in the Book of Jashar," sometimes translated as "The Book of the Upright." The same book, perhaps a collection of poetic hero stories, is also quoted in Joshua 10:12-13, and it seems to have been widely known.

Scholars generally assume that "bow" refers to the tune, or perhaps the title of the dirge, along the lines of superscriptions to some of the psalms. Thus, some translations insert "song of" before "the bow" (NRSV, NASB, HCSB), or put "The Bow" in quotation marks (NET).

The lament itself consists of two unequal stanzas (vv. 20-24 and vv. 25b-26) framed by the threefold refrain, "How the mighty have fallen!" (vv. 19, 25a, 27). The first stanza is a tribute to Saul, beginning with an enigmatic exclamation, literally, "The gazelle of Israel upon the high places is slain." The image of the king as a proud gazelle lying dead on a high crag is sad indeed. The word for "gazelle" could also mean "beauty" or "glory," however, so most translations have something like "Your glory, O Israel" (NRSV, NIV) or "Your beauty, O Israel" (NASB), deleting the article and adding "your." The NET has "The beauty of Israel . . . ."

The dirge takes the form of what rhetoricians call an "apostrophe," as it is addressed to various people or things, none of whom are present. "Tell it not in Gath, proclaim it not in the streets of Ashkelon" (v. 20) would have been directed to Philistine messengers sent to declare the news in their chief cities. David could not bear the thought of Philistine maidens singing and dancing over the news that Saul was dead in the same way that Israelite maidens sang in celebration when Saul and David returned from killing Philistines (1 Sam 18:6-7).

From the absent Philistines, David turns to address the mountains of the Gilboa range, calling for the dew and rain to leave dry the place where Saul's blood was spilled, and where he imagined that Saul's shield lay in the dust (v. 21). Shields were typically made of thick leather, sometimes with added metal plates. The leather was rubbed with oil to keep it from cracking, and perhaps to make the surface more slippery and better able to deflect enemy blows. The double entendre in the phrase "anointed with oil no more" is no doubt intentional: Israel's anointed one is no longer alive to anoint his shield.

David praises the fighting prowess and fierce loyalty of Saul and Jonathan in v. 22: Saul's sword and Jonathan's bow did not turn back "from the blood of the slain, from the fat of the mighty," a graphic depiction of the pair's martial talent and tenacity. The claim that they were "not divided" in life or in death (v. 23) reflects some hyperbole because Jonathan's partiality to David had caused severe friction between him and his father. Even so, Jonathan remained faithful to his father rather than defecting with David.

As much as David despised the thought of "the daughters of the Philistines" celebrating Saul's death (v. 20), he called upon "the daughters of Israel" to weep for Saul as if he had personally provided them with luxurious adornments (v. 24).

While David mourns Saul as a champion in the first stanza, he grieves for Jonathan as a friend. The second stanza is shorter than the first, but even more plaintive and personal:

> I am distressed for you, my brother Jonathan;
> greatly beloved were you to me;
> your love to me was wonderful,
> passing the love of women. (1:26)

The friendship between David and Jonathan is a common theme in 1 Samuel. Most often (1 Sam 18:1-5; 19:1; 20:17), Jonathan is more demonstrative in expressing his affection for David, and one might gather that the relationship was one-sided, but the story of their parting in 1 Sam 20:42 stresses the depth of David's love for Jonathan. There, David prostrates himself before his friend and embraces him. They both weep, but the text implies that David weeps more (literally, in the context of weeping, "David made great").

It should come as no surprise that v. 26 has given rise to considerable speculation that the two shared a homosexual relationship. Arguments to that end are unconvincing, however. In an anthrocentric age when men typically married for sex, children, and household labor, their best friends were likely other men, not their wives. Both David and Jonathan were married with children, and David's attraction to women (see 2 Sam 11) is legendary. David's celebration of the bond he shared with Jonathan does not necessarily bear sexual overtones.

As the elegy began, so it ended with the plaintive, "How the mighty have fallen!" David's earnest expression of grief and his skillful handling of the situation allowed him to accept the emblems of Saul's kingship without appearing to have sought them, and to reinforce the respect that Israel should pay to the anointed of God. David's anointing by Samuel was not public knowledge, but it would become known in due time, and there would be more official anointings as well (2 Sam 2:4; 5:3).

David would soon be king of all Israel.

Lamentation and Learning

The painful account found in 2 Samuel 1 suggests several points to ponder. One relates to integrity: the reader suspects that the Amalekite who brought David Saul's crown had no integrity. When he prostrated himself before David and spun a tale about how he "just happened" to come upon Saul, he was more interested in personal rewards than in telling the truth. In contrast, when David adopted a mourning posture for Saul and Jonathan—though their deaths helped him reach the throne—his grief was genuine. In both sorrow and joy, God's people are called to lives of integrity.

David's judgment on the Amalekite reflects the truth that when we sin, we bring judgment on ourselves. Someone else may declare our guilt or pronounce our penalty, but when we do wrong, the fault is our own. We may choose to do evil or good. We may choose to repent and reform, or not. We live in a culture of blame in which it's easy to lay our failures at the feet of parents or peers. While we cannot and should not deny the influence of our environment, at some point we must recognize that we are responsible for our own behavior.

David's unashamed mourning for Saul and Jonathan offers a helpful example of healthy grief. Many of us, especially men, are conditioned to keep our emotions in check. While the discipline to manage our emotions is good, we must be careful not to stifle or deny our feelings. When sad times come—and they will, for all of us—we need to grieve. David expressed his grief in physical ways that were appropriate to his culture, ripping his raiment and wailing aloud—notably in the presence of "all the men who were with him" (v. 11). He also thought through his sorrow, shaping it into the words of a touching and elegant elegy for those he had loved and lost (vv. 19-27). Expressing our feelings both alone and in the company of friends is good medicine. Journaling or putting our feelings into a poem or song can be highly cathartic.

Giving vent to our grief on tragic days helps us to absorb the shock of loss and move through it, rather than bottling our pain and getting emotionally stuck. Big boys—and girls—*do* cry.

1. Do you think the Amalekite in 1 Samuel 1 was telling the truth or twisting it to his advantage? Why?

_____

_____

_____

_____

_____

2. It's often tempting for us to "stretch the truth" or lie outright in hopes of avoiding trouble or gaining an advantage. How important is truth-telling to you?

_____

_____

_____

_____

_____

3. Do you live up to the standards you expect of others?

_____

_____

_____

_____

_____

4. Can you think of times—as a child, youth, or adult—when you did something wrong but sought to avoid responsibility by blaming someone else for it?

_____

_____

_____

_____

_____

5. What message did you receive about crying when you were a child? Were you encouraged to express your emotions or to "keep a stiff upper lip" and maintain control at all times?

_____

_____

_____

_____

_____

6. Children learn by example as much as by word. Did you ever see your parents cry? Have your children ever seen you weeping?

_____

_____

_____

_____

_____

7. How can we exercise appropriate concern about upsetting children or others, while also giving ourselves freedom to grieve?

_____

_____

_____

_____

_____

8. Think about a great loss you have experienced: the death of a loved one, the death of a relationship, the loss of a job, the loss of innocence. How did you deal with your grief?

_____

_____

_____

_____

_____

9. What cathartic measures do you take when dealing with grief? Keeping a journal? Talking with friends? Pouring yourself into an art or building project? Praying? What is most effective for you?

_____

_____

_____

_____

_____

My House, Your House

2 Samuel 7:1-29

Have you ever made big plans for a special project or trip and had them turned upside down? Normally we would consider that a negative experience. For David, however, a major change in plans turned out to be a blessing beyond his wildest dreams.

A Busy King

Imagine what it would be like to sit where King David sat in the early years of his reign in Jerusalem. Perhaps he was seated in his new house one day, or maybe even reclining, when a new thought popped into King David's head: *he had time to sit*, time to think, time to plan ahead. That was something new for David. From the day God called him from following the sheep of his father Jesse until now, there had been precious little time to sit or rest or think about anything beyond daily survival. David's life was a whirlwind for years.

There was a time when life was simpler, when he tended sheep for his father, but David was called from the peaceful pastures around Bethlehem to join King Saul's court in Gibeah. The text suggests that David first served Saul as his personal musician, then as his personal bodyguard, or armor bearer. He served Israel by defeating Goliath and proving himself as a military leader. He served God by remaining faithful and trusting the Lord when others around him were lost in fear.

But King Saul soon grew jealous of David's success. Steeped in paranoia and troubled by an "evil spirit," Saul tried to kill David on multiple occasions, and things got so bad that David had to run for his life. For years he lived in the bleak wilderness of the southern Negeb, leading a band of social outcasts and renegade slaves, ever watchful for Saul's continued pursuit. Along the way, David married at least two different women. David was busy.

Eventually, David had to resort to hiding out among the Philistines, feigning fealty to King Achish in order to escape King Saul. There David and his men made their living by raiding the towns and villages of some of Israel's old enemies, leaving little time for relaxation.

David's life grew even busier when King Saul and his three strongest sons were killed in a great battle on Mount Gilboa. That created a power vacuum in Israel, and David was destined to fill it. The people living in Judah soon called for him to become king over Judah, and they crowned him at Hebron (2 Sam 2:4).

Saul's general Abner had maintained a shadow government in northern Israel for two years, using Ishboshet (also called Ishbaal), Saul's least competent son, as a puppet king. With David ruling Judah and Abner calling the shots in Israel, there was war between the north and the south. In time, however, David's general Joab murdered Abner (2 Sam 3:26-30) in blood vengeance for having killed his brother Asahel in battle (2 Sam 2:18-23), and Ishbosheth was assassinated by a couple of rogues (2 Sam 4:5-8). David had to make slick political maneuvers to avoid blame for either death, but he was so successful that the elders of the northern tribes came to Hebron and agreed to anoint him king of Israel, allowing David to unite all the tribes of Israel under a single monarchy.

This business kept David on the go, though he managed to sire sons by six different wives (2 Sam 3:1-5). He had to be constantly on guard for political intrigue and the possibility of attempts on his own life. He had to improve relations with former enemies who were now his subjects. He had to set up the structure for an entirely new system of government. There was precious little time for rest.

David recognized the political advantages of establishing his capital in neutral territory, so he led his army to conquer the city of Jerusalem, a Jebusite stronghold that had never been defeated (2 Sam 5:6-10). On that small mountain, located near the intersection of northern and southern Israel, he set up his government and began to build a city to call his own.

David was able to establish peaceful alliances with other surrounding kingdoms through skillful political moves, including intermarriage with the daughters of neighboring kingdoms. King Hiram of Tyre, Israel's immediate neighbor to the north, was so impressed by David that he sent his own craftsmen and materials to build David a palace of cedar and stone (2 Sam 5:11-16). Israel's neighbors were not content to let him rest in peace, however. The Philistines attacked more than once, but David was able to rally his troops and defeat the opponents soundly (2 Sam 5:17-25).

Once the political and military situations stabilized, David shrewdly worked to establish Jerusalem as the religious center of Israel, too. He went to great effort to bring the Ark of the Covenant into Jerusalem, where he housed it in a special tent made of heavy curtains (2 Samuel 6).

So it was that for these many years, David's life was a whirlwind of activity, always teetering on the brink of grave danger and in need of constant attention . . . until the day David woke up and realized there was no pressing issue to deal with that day. No Philistines threatened the gates, no Egyptian emissaries wanted to talk trade, no cabinet ministers pleaded for his help with the national debt. The text says, "the king was settled in his palace and the LORD had given him rest from all his enemies around him" (v. 1).

A Thoughtful King

Finally, David had time to sit and think. To think about where he was and how he got there. To think about what he had done and who had helped him. To think about what lay ahead and how he would get there. There came a day when David was overwhelmed by a single thought: "Here I am, living in a palace of cedar, while the ark of God remains in a tent" (v. 2).

David suddenly saw the incongruity of enjoying his own fine house while the Ark of the Covenant, where Yahweh was thought to dwell above the cherubim, was still consigned to a tent. It was a big, fancy, colorful tent, befitting the name "tabernacle," but it was a tent nonetheless.

David knew that everything he had accomplished was due to the power of God at work within him. Yahweh gave him strength to overcome lions and bears while he kept his father's flocks. Yahweh gave him the courage and skill to defeat Goliath and spark Israel's victory over the Philistines. Yahweh gave him favor in Saul's eyes, and Yahweh later protected him from Saul's jealousy. Yahweh aided David in the wilderness and ultimately gave him the kingdom.

It was customary in the ancient world for kings to build an impressive temple to the national god as one of their first acts. Such temples served not only to demonstrate royal piety, but also to centralize royal power. In the minds of the people, gods such as Marduk or Ishtar or Dagon or Baal dwelt in the house that the king built for them, establishing a strong bond between god and king.

David, like all other kings of the ancient world, wanted to demonstrate his love for the god who had blessed him. Certainly, he was not ignorant of the political advantages of such a move. But David also appears motivated by a genuine sense of respect and reverence for God. It didn't seem right to him that he lived in a fine cedar house while Yahweh lived in a portable tent. So he thought, "I will build a house for Yahweh."

David knew, however, that you can't build something on that scale without a building permit, and one had to acquire temple permits from God himself. David took his plans to Nathan, who is first mentioned here, and who seems to have served as David's official court prophet and thus his primary liaison with Yahweh. Nathan thought David's plan sounded like a great idea, and he encouraged David to do whatever was in his heart (2 Sam 7:2-3).

An Awesome God

But that night, Nathan could not sleep. David had found rest, but Nathan had lost it. Nathan realized that a prophet can speak too soon. In a vision of the night, God sent a surprising message:

> Go and tell my servant David, "This is what the LORD says: Are *you* the one to build *me* a house to dwell in? I have not dwelt in a house from the day I brought the Israelites up out of Egypt to this day. I have been moving from place to place with a tent as my dwelling. Wherever I have moved with all the Israelites, did I ever say to any of their rulers whom I commanded to shepherd my people Israel, 'Why have you not built me a house of cedar?'" (2 Sam 5:5-7, my emphasis)

Yahweh's question, "Did I ever live in a house before?" implies that the Ark had always remained in a tent. There was a period, however, when the Ark was in the temple at Shiloh, and it was called a *house* (*bayit*), but evidently that was considered a temporary stopover, like the twenty years in Abinadab's house in Kiriathjearim, or the three months in Obed Edom's house just before arriving in Jerusalem. Or perhaps God was pointing out that where the Ark of the Covenant dwells and where God dwells are not necessarily the same.

In short, Yahweh's message to David was, "Thanks, but no thanks. I don't need a house." Rather, God gave Nathan a message for David that reminded the king of how he had been blessed and promised even more:

> This is what the LORD Almighty says: I took you from the pasture and from following the flock to be ruler over my people Israel. I have been with you wherever you have gone, and I have cut off all your enemies from before you. Now I will make your name great, like the names of the greatest men of the earth. And I will provide a place for my people Israel and will plant them so that they can have a home of their own and no longer be disturbed. Wicked people will not oppress them anymore, as they did at the beginning and have done ever since the time I appointed leaders over my people Israel. I will also give you rest from all your enemies. (2 Sam 7:8b-11a)

Take note of the emphatic use of the first person, as Yahweh spoke of past activity and future promises on David's behalf: "I took you from the pasture . . . ," "I have been with you . . . ," "I have cut off your enemies . . . ," "Now I will make your name great . . . ," "I will provide a place for my people Israel . . . ," "I will also give you rest" (2 Sam 7:8b-11a). Although David had been a busy man, Yahweh had blessed his work and would continue to do so. But there was more to God's message, amazingly more, a promise so important that I quote it in full:

> The LORD declares to you that the LORD himself will establish a house for you: When your days are over and you rest with your fathers, I will raise up your offspring to succeed you, who will come from your own body, and I will establish his kingdom. He is the one who will build a house for my Name, and I will establish the throne of his kingdom forever. I will be his father, and he will be my son. When he does wrong, I will punish him with the rod of men, with floggings inflicted by men. But my love will never be taken away from him, as I took it away from Saul, whom I removed from before you. Your house and your kingdom will endure forever before me; your throne will be established forever. (2 Sam 7:11b-16)

Don't miss the metaphor: the entire story turns on the use of a marvelous and powerful play on words that we can paraphrase as "I don't need you to build me a house, David. I will build *you* a house." The word "house" has a double meaning. David wanted to build for Yahweh a house of wood and stone and mortar. God wanted to build for David a house of security in which his descendants would rule Israel forever. David wanted to build Yahweh a temple. God wanted to build David a dynasty.

That was an incredible turn of events. What began as an act of personal piety and political power was transformed into a promise of divine and unconditional grace. We should not overlook the significance of this event: We can see Nathan's dynastic oracle in 2 Samuel 7 as the turning point, not only of the Deuteronomistic history, but of the entire Old Testament.

This chapter, *this* text is the foundation of the theological bridge that leads from law to grace. *This* story of God and David is the first step on a new path that leads ultimately to the story of Jesus and all the undeserving Davids in the world. *This* account is at the root of all evangelical theology, for it is the beginning of the gospel.

To this point, God's relationship with Israel was one of master and servant. It was a conditional relationship in which God was faithful, but his blessings were dependent on Israel's obedience, and the Israelites were no more inclined to obedience than we are. Read the book of Deuteronomy. Read Joshua. Read Judges. Read 1 Samuel. It is the same story told time and again in different ways. When Israel is obedient, God's blessings are abundant. When Israel rebels, God is not to be found. The relationship between God and his people always seems to turn on the word "*if.*"

But now things are changing. With God's covenant promise to David, a new element enters the picture. It is the element of grace. In this covenant with David, God makes a promise that is not ultimately conditioned by David's obedience or the obedience of his children. Rather, it is an unconditional promise of undeserved grace. Yahweh will bless David's house and establish his dynasty upon the throne. If David's descendants prove to be disobedient, God will allow them to experience the natural effects of their sin— "punishment with the rods of men" is the way he puts it—but God will never withdraw his steadfast covenant love.

When Saul disobeyed one time too many, Yahweh cut him off and withdrew his spirit. But for David, there was something new. In essence, God declared, "Disobedience will buy you trouble, but I will never cut you off. Your house and your kingdom will endure forever before me; your throne will be established forever." The operative conjunction has been changed from "if" to "nevertheless." God promised that his choice of David's descendants as the leaders and agents of salvation for Israel would never change.

What do we make of this promise, since we know the Davidic kingdom did not, in fact, last forever? The kingdom of Judah endured 150 years longer than the northern kingdom, but it also came to a full stop in 586 BC, when Jerusalem burned to the ground. King Jeconiah, the last descendant of David with rights to the throne, was carried in chains to Babylon a decade before. Yet, God's promise was not violated. When God's people became corrupt and fell prey to their own weakness, they were chastised with the rods of men just as Nathan predicted. The men just happened to be Babylonians.

But God never left his people. God never forgot them. The burning of God's temple and the loss of its contents had no effect on the presence of God with Israel. The Lord went with his people into exile and offered hope through the prophetic words of Jeremiah and Ezekiel and Second Isaiah. After fifty years of exile, God used Cyrus the Persian as the agent of change who would conquer Babylon and allow the Jews to return to Jerusalem. Some did. Some did not. Yet God remained with all of them.

That was part of what the Lord wanted David to understand. God cannot be limited to one place, to one king, to one people. God cannot be housebroken or fenced in. God will be free, or else he is not God at all.

An Eternal House

It was in such freedom that God chose to enter our world in a new way, through the person of a man named Jesus, descended of the house and lineage of David. In Jesus Christ, God completed the work of amazing grace that began in the Old Testament and runs into the New. Through the life and work and death and resurrection of Jesus, God offers salvation that is not predicated on our works or our perfect obedience, but on the grace of God alone.

Our hope in God is not based on a human "if," but on a divine "nevertheless." Even though we are weak, even though we fail, even though we fall short of God's ideal, God loves us still. God forgives us still.

It is not up to us to build God a house in which to dwell. Rather, God's purpose is to build a house for us—a family of faith in which we may find forgiveness and acceptance and strength for every day. Paul spoke of how God's power works within us "to accomplish abundantly far more than all we can ask or imagine" (Eph 3:20). We also may sin, and may be subject to the earthly consequences of our sin, but that is not the end. God loves us *nevertheless*. The key to joyful and productive Christian living is not found in a legalistic gospel of how much we do for God, but how much we allow God to do for us.

Now, just as God promised to David that his descendants would rule forever, so we believe that God in Christ rules forever and that God's promises extend for all time. God has built a house for us. When the disciples mourned that Jesus was leaving them, he told them not to worry. "In my Father's house are many rooms," he said. "I'm going to prepare a place for you" (John 14:1-3).

What an amazing love and grace! When Nathan brought the word of God to David, the king was so overcome that he went straight to the tabernacle and seated himself before the Ark of the Covenant, where he believed the presence of God was strongest. There he offered an amazed, effusive, and somewhat repetitive prayer of praise (2 Sam 7:18-29), and the heart of his prayer was this: "Because of your promise, and according to your own heart, *you* have wrought all this greatness, so that your servant may know it. Therefore, your are great, O LORD God; for there is none like you, and there is no God besides you . . . " (2 Sam 7:21-22, my emphasis).

David's story demands that we consider our own response to God's promises. How will we respond to the awesome, amazing grace of God? Will we remain stuck in the rut of trying to earn God's favor by building a house of good works, or will we accept the house of grace and promise that God has already built for us? Grace awaits, and it is amazing indeed.

1. The visionary message Nathan delivered recited a number of ways in which God had blessed David. Name some of the ways you believe God has blessed you.

_____

_____

_____

_____

_____

2. David wanted to build a house for God. Christians today often refer to their churches as a "house of God." Sometimes churches spend exorbitant amounts of money on sanctuaries and buildings, believing that doing so gives greater glory to God. How does that reasoning square with God's insistence to David that God doesn't need a house?

_____

_____

_____

_____

_____

3. Perhaps you, like David, have wanted to do something special for God. What kind of actions, based on the full biblical witness, do you believe will be most pleasing in God's sight?

_____

_____

_____

_____

_____

4. Have you ever made specific commitments to do something for God? To attend church, perhaps, or tithe, or raise your children in a Christian home? What specific promises to God have you made?

_____

_____

_____

_____

_____

5. What are some promises that you believe God has made to you?

_____

_____

_____

_____

_____

My House, Your House

6. Can any of the things you do for God make God love you more? If not, what is your motivation for doing them?

_____

_____

_____

_____

_____

One Thing Leads to Another

2 Samuel 12:1-25

Do you like surprises? Do you like stories? A quick study of
2 Samuel 12 shows that it contains both a story and a surprise, but
the intended recipient didn't like either one. You wouldn't have,
either.

David's Downfall

The text before us follows one of the most disappointing stories in
the entire Bible: after many years of living faithfully before God and
rising to become a model king over Israel, David's train fell off the
tracks. The text implies that David may have grown complacent: 2
Samuel 1-10 describes, in almost breathless fashion, how David
exercised political skill and charismatic leadership to become king
over all Israel, how he defeated enemies all around, how he organized his government and settled into his role as monarch. The
narrator frequently points out how David sought Yahweh's direction
before taking actions (1 Sam 23:2, 4; 30:8; 2 Sam 2:1; 5:19, 23),
and that David's various successes were due to Yahweh's blessing (1
Sam 24:10; 26:23; 2 Sam 5:12; 8:6, 14).

After some time, however, there came a spring when the
Ammonites threatened. It was "the time of the year when kings go
out to battle," but the king decided instead to send Joab to lead the
army, and "David remained in Jerusalem" (2 Sam 11:1). While tar-
rying in Jerusalem, resting on his rooftop patio and ogling a woman
at her bath, David fell victim to the only enemy he could not defeat:
himself. We know what happened next: David sent for Bathsheba
and began a sexual relationship (whether consensual or coercive, we
do not know) that culminated in a pregnancy. Trying to hide his sin,
David called Bathsheba's husband Uriah home from the battle in

hopes that he would sleep with his wife. When Uriah—one of David's most loyal and valiant soldiers—refused to break his holy war vow of purity, David sent him back to the front bearing a sealed message containing his death warrant. Joab read the message, sent Uriah into the thickest part of battle, and pulled back other supporting troops, leaving Uriah to die at the hands of the Ammonites.

But it was really David's hand that did the deed. David told Joab not to worry about it, literally, "do not let this matter be evil in your eyes" (11:25), but the closing phrase of the chapter reveals how backwards David's thinking had become. Connecting David's and Yahweh's words in an artful way that is unfortunately glossed over by the NRSV and most modern translations, the narrator concludes, "But the thing that David did was evil in the eyes of Yahweh . . ." (11:27b).

Nathan's Parable (12:1-6)

The narrator's judgment of what David did in 11:27b serves also as an adroit transition to the next chapter, for it is grammatically connected to the opening words of 12:1 (". . . and Yahweh sent Nathan to David").

The prophet Nathan first appears in 2 Samuel 7, where he speaks Yahweh's promise to establish for David a dynastic house destined to rule over Israel forever. One would assume, then, that Nathan was in good standing with the king, with ready access to David's ear. Thus, David was unsuspecting when Nathan's visit turned out to be a much heavier interview than he expected.

Despite the linguistic bond between chapters 11 and 12, the reader is to assume that some time passed since David's initial act of adultery and conspiracy in the death of Bathsheba's husband. We learn from 11:26-27a that following Uriah's death and a suitable period of mourning for her husband (seven days, at least), Bathsheba moved to the palace at David's behest, officially became one of his wives, and bore him a son. So we may assume that David's sinful actions were many months behind him. Perhaps he thought he had gotten away with murder.

Nathan's visit would soon remove any such illusions. His message to David is in the form of a juridical parable that proposes a conflicted situation and asks the hearer to pass judgment (compare 2 Sam 14:1-20; 1 Kgs 20:39-40; Isa 5:1-7).

Nathan told a story of two different men. One was rich, powerful, and arrogant. The other was poor, helpless, and humble. The rich man had more livestock than he could count, while the poor man had only one lamb, which he loved like a child. When the wealthy man was obligated to entertain an unexpected visitor, he sent a servant to steal the poor man's lamb, slaughter it, and feed it to his guest (vv. 2-4).

The characters are so clearly drawn and the rich man's behavior so contemptible that "David's anger was greatly kindled against the man," and with an oath formula ("As the Lord lives . . ."), he condemned the selfish thief (v. 5). Modern translations such as NRSV attribute to David the words "the one who has done this deserves to die!" but the literal meaning is "a son of death is the man who did this!" It is possible that "son of death" was intended as a negative epithet similar to the phrase "son of Belial" or "son of worthlessness," translated as "scoundrel" in 2 Samuel 16:7 and 20:1.

Reading "son of death" as an invective avoids the difficult problem of whether David declared two dissimilar sentences, for in v. 6 he pronounces a financial penalty, calling for the guilty party to restore the stolen lamb fourfold. This would have been in keeping with the law in Exodus 22:1, which set the penalty for sheep stealing as a fourfold restitution.

The Prophet's Point (12:7-15)

After waiting for David to be suitably enraged by the protagonist's injustice, Nathan was ready to ensure that David got the point of his story, probably at the end of the prophet's pointed finger: *"You are the man!"*

With that simple accusation, the crestfallen king's own words of judgment came to roost on his own head. Speaking in Yahweh's behalf, Nathan used a striking combination of first person and second person verbs to clarify the full measure of David's sin, which was not against Bathsheba and Uriah only, but against God: "*I* anointed you king over Israel; *I* rescued you from the hand of Saul; *I* gave you your master's house, and your master's wives into your bosom, and gave you the house of Israel and of Judah; and if that had been too little, *I* would have added as much more" (vv. 7-8).

Full in the face of God's constant blessings, however, David chose to go his own way. "Why have you despised the word of the LORD," Nathan asked, "to do what is evil in his sight?" (note the literary link back to 11:25 and 27). "*You* have struck down Uriah the Hittite with the sword, and have taken his wife to be your wife, and have killed him with the sword of the Ammonites" (v. 9).

One Thing Leads to Another

In v. 10, a third person verb marks the transition from accusation to judgment ("Now therefore the sword shall never depart from your house"), but the narrator quickly shifts back to second person verbs to repeat David's crime ("for you have despised me, and have taken the wife of Uriah the Hittite to be your wife"). Then the narrator moves to first person verbs to show that Yahweh will wield the punishing blade: "*I* will raise up trouble against you from within your own house; and I will take your wives before your eyes, and give them to your neighbor, and he shall lie with your wives in the sight of this very sun" (v. 11). David committed his sin in secret, but his punishment would be a matter of public record (v. 12).

Nathan's reference to anointing probably speaks of Samuel's secretive actions in 1 Sam 16:13 more than the two official ceremonies described in 2 Saml 2:4 and 5:3. The point is that *Yahweh*, not just popular acclaim, was the source of David's rise to the throne. On a side note, v. 8 provides our only textual evidence that David took Saul's small harem for himself. In context, Saul's wives appear in a series of deific gifts designed to emphasize Yahweh's generosity.

Nathan's reference to the "word of the LORD" (v. 9) recalled the Law of Moses. David had violated the commandments against coveting, adultery, theft, and murder. Enough time had passed for the child conceived in David's sin to be born, but if David thought his despicable deeds were forgotten or overlooked, he was mistaken. Nathan's fiery charges targeted David's evil in no uncertain terms. The accusation of murder is unmistakable: twice he accused David of killing Uriah with the sword of the Ammonites ("sword" is metaphorical; according to 11:24, Uriah was killed by Ammonite archers).

Nathan built on the sword metaphor with a prediction that David, who had previously benefited from God's blessings, was now destined to experience divine retribution (v. 10). "I will raise up trouble against you from within your own house" (v. 11a) may be seen as a prediction of the tragic and bitter events that unfold in ensuing chapters, culminating in public humiliation for the king, the rape of David's daughter, and the deaths of three sons.

Some later rabbis drew a connection between David's call for fourfold restitution and tragedies affecting four of his children: the death of Bathsheba's firstborn son, the rape of his daughter Tamar, and the deaths of his sons Amnon (murdered by his half-brother

"An innocent shall die for the guilty."

Absalom) and Absalom (who died while leading a rebellion against his father). Although their surmise is interesting, David's penalty was much broader.

Nathan's cutting words had their intended effect, though David's response is downplayed to keep the spotlight on God's spokesman. "I have sinned against the LORD" was all David managed to say. Despite the king's paltry show of penitence, Nathan declared that Yahweh had put away David's sin. The grace David received, however, would not come cheaply. David's guilt did not simply disappear as a result of divine forbearance; he had "utterly scorned the LORD," and his sin could not be easily dismissed. Rather than falling upon David, however, the penalty David deserved (Lev 20:10; Deut 22:22) was transferred to the innocent offspring of his adultery, as Nathan announced: "the child that is born to you shall die" (v. 14). The caustic term David had used to describe the greedy landowner came back to haunt him, for Bathsheba's baby boy was doomed to be a "son of death."

A Death and a Birth (12:15b-25)

Nathan's funereal forecast suggested that the child, a living reminder of David's wrongdoing, would die in David's place. The narrator underscores David's guilt by eschewing Bathsheba's name and speaking of her only as "Uriah's wife."

Readers often assume the child was a newborn who was ill from birth and lived only seven days, but the text does not support this. The baby's birth is reported in 11:27, with no indication of frailty. The narration suggests that the boy enjoyed an unknown period of health before Yahweh "struck the child" in fulfillment of Nathan's prophecy.

David's prayerful reaction to the child's illness stands in striking contrast to the brevity of his confession. As the child grew progressively ill over seven days, David's agitated and single-minded behavior was a living conundrum in the eyes of the royal household, who may have thought he was overreacting. But David knew something his administrative officials and household staff did not know: he alone knew that the child did not suffer from a normal disease, but from the deadly weight of his father's sin.

All too aware of his guilt, David pleaded with God for the child's life, refused to eat any food, and spent each night lying on the floor, presumably by the child's bed (v. 16). David's prayerful performance was so painful that his court counselors pleaded with him to get up and comport himself in a more regal fashion, but he would not (v. 17). More than health and dignity were involved, however: David's refusal to sit at the royal table is an indication that he also remained aloof from matters of state and protocol.

When Yahweh did not respond to David's prayer and the child died, the king's demeanor changed radically. Aware that his best efforts had failed and there was nothing more he could do to save the child, David bathed and dressed, went to worship in the temple, then returned to the everyday world of taking his meals and attending to business (v. 20).

David had unleashed such depth of emotion during the child's illness that the servants had been afraid to tell him when the child died (vv. 18-19), so they were shocked when he received the news dispassionately and then refused to join the official mourning after the boy's death. This aroused such consternation among observers that even his servants reproved him (v. 21), but David explained that he had done his grieving in advance: now that the child was dead, he saw no need to continue (vv. 22-23).

David's week of fasting and prayer seems to have served as a proleptic period of mourning. The normal season of grief in Israel was seven days, and that is how long David had already wept for the life of the little one. When his self-abasement proved fruitless, David refused to mourn any longer.

The narrator seems to have understood the child's death as an indication that God's displeasure with David's marriage to Bathsheba had been put in the past. He no longer refers to Bathsheba as "Uriah's wife," but calls her by name or describes her as David's wife. Thus we read that, though David did not join the public mourning, "he consoled his wife Bathsheba" in his own way, and soon she became pregnant again—with the child who would be named Solomon.

On the surface, it seems strange that the birth story of a king so eminent as Solomon emerged from the shadow of Nathan's curse. Perhaps the narrator wants to emphasize that, though Yahweh did not answer David's plea to save the first child, God showed abundant grace through granting another son. Later readers would need to hear that hope survives in the midst of darkness, that bleak and noisome days can give birth to hope: a new son was born, and "The LORD loved him."

Solomon's name may mean "man of peace" (see 1 Chr 22:9), or possibly "one who makes complete" (i.e., "replacement"). Of more interest, however, is a second name: Nathan declared that Yahweh had called the child "Jedidiah," meaning "Beloved One of Yahweh." One would think such a memorable name would prove popular, but it does not appear again in the Bible.

The brevity of Solomon's birth story sharpens the contrast between him and his ill-fated brother, placing him clearly in the bright (if small) spotlight. The first son of Bathsheba was both unnamed and unfortunate, cursed by Yahweh with his father's sin. In contrast, Solomon is twice named and clearly blessed by Yahweh, whose love for the child is stated by the narrator, announced by the prophet Nathan, and signified by the name Jedidiah.

A Troublesome Tale

What shall we do with a story like this? The notion that God would punish David by taking the life of an innocent child is unsettling and will leave any sensitive reader with a level of discomfort regarding the state of divine ethics. Did God kill Bathsheba's baby because of David's sin? That is what the narrator and apparently the prophet Nathan believed. We might not be as inclined to interpret the child's death in the same way, but the queasy feeling it gives us can serve another purpose, for it reminds us of a New Testament story that also involves rebellious people and an innocent son dying for others.

The two stories are not the same: unlike David's child, who had no choice in the matter, Jesus willingly chose to give his life for the sake of others. David's long lamentation, however, reminds us that the death of a child constitutes the worst pain a parent can know. Perhaps David's grief can also suggest some small insight into what God the Father may have experienced with regard to the New Testament story in which "God so loved the world that he gave his only son . . ." (John 3:16).

David's repetitive petitions also remind us that prayers aren't always answered in the way we hope. When asked to explain his behavior, David told his counselors, "While the child was still alive, I fasted and wept; for I said, 'Who knows? The LORD may be gracious to me, and the child may live'" (v. 22).

David was not alone in such pondering relative to the profit of prayer. The book of Jonah claims that when faced with the prophet's message of doom, the king of Ninevah called for widespread repentance, saying, "Who knows? God may relent and change his mind; he may turn from his fierce anger, so that we do not perish" (Jonah

3:9). Joel offered the same hope when pleading with the Hebrews to repent: "Who knows whether he will turn and relent, and leave a blessing behind him . . . ?" (Joel 2:14). Texts like these may seem troubling, but they offer a balancing corrective to others who seem to guarantee that faithful prayers will gain the blessing we seek (1 Chr 4:10; Jas 5:13-17). God respects our prayers but always remains free to act as God wills.

The painful aspects of 2 Samuel 12 can be deeply troubling, but hope was born in the midst of the trouble, and Solomon, whose name is derived from *shalom*, became a sign of the peace and wholeness God desires to give. Although only Solomon was given the name "Jedidiah," we are reminded that all people are beloved of God.

1. David thought the rich man in Nathan's story was a poor excuse for a human being. What do you think? Can you imagine any rationalization for his behavior?

_____

_____

_____

_____

_____

2. David's sins in 2 Samuel 11 illustrate the truth that one thing leads to another. Think of other illustrations of how one sin can lead to greater sin and greater sorrow.

_____

_____

_____

_____

_____

3. Ultimately, sin leads to death (Rom 6:23), and not always of the sinner alone. The death that comes through sin may be physical, or it may be the death of relationships, of good health, of a career, of hope. Can you think of ways in which you have experienced death as a result of sin?

_____

_____

_____

_____

4. Some might argue that, if we are not guaranteed a positive answer to our prayers, there's no point in praying. What do you think?

_____

_____

_____

_____

_____

5. Does the death of Bathsheba's first son—and the birth of a second who was called "beloved of Yahweh"—suggest that God did not love the child who died?

_____

_____

_____

_____

_____

6. Can you think of another instance in which an innocent child died for the sake of someone else's sin?

_____

_____

_____

_____

_____

One Thing Leads to Another

Days of Their Lives

2 Samuel 15:13–19:8

People who enjoy soap operas should love the extended drama found in 2 Samuel 13–19. David could have called it *All My Children*. It is filled with *The Young and the Restless*, as well as *The Bold and the Beautiful*, and frequently in need of a *General Hospital*. There is sex here, and violence, and sometimes the two of them together. There are family problems and hidden plots, political shenanigans and a flaunting of authority. This was a soap opera before there was soap to sell.

The stories we find in 2 Sam 13:1–19:8 constitute a single literary unit devoted to the greatest political crisis of David's career—the rebellion led by his own son Absalom. Both individual elements and the story as a whole are portrayed as the fulfillment of Nathan's prophecy to David that, due to his adultery with Bathsheba and the murder of her husband Uriah, "the sword shall never depart from your house" (12:10). A quick look at the entire section will help us understand the consequences of David's actions. We'll give a bit more attention to the latter section.

Amnon and Tamar (13:1-22)

Amnon was David's firstborn son, the daughter of Ahinoam of Jezreel (1 Sam 25:43; 2 Sam 3:2). His name means "to be faithful," but his character did not match his name. Amnon had the misfortune of falling in lust with his half-sister Tamar, the daughter of David by Maacah, a princess from Geshur who was probably married to David to seal a political alliance (see 2 Sam 3:3). The narrator introduces the story of Amnon and Tamar by pointing out that *Absalom* had a sister named Tamar, a literary indication that Absalom will overshadow all that follows.

Amnon was frustrated because virgin daughters of the king were probably confined to a special section of the palace and guarded closely, so he could not get to the object of his affection. Amnon took his friend Jonadab's crafty advice and feigned illness, requesting that Tamar nurse him back to health by cooking special cakes for him ("dumplings" might be a better translation, since the dish was boiled).

Whether there was ever mutual attraction between Amnon and Tamar is unclear. Consanguinity between siblings of different mothers apparently was allowed during that period, and at one point (albeit under threat of rape), Tamar suggested the possibility of their marriage.

Amnon, however, thought only of sex and power and violence, not necessarily in that order. Tamar pleaded with him that he not bring shame to her and disgrace upon himself, but he was not dissuaded, and he forcibly raped her.

Tamar is thus remembered as a tragic victim: because she was no longer a virgin, she was no longer a candidate for a royal marriage, and thus doomed to live as a widow for the rest of her life. Amnon fully earned his later reputation as a despicable boor. Having raped his sister, his reputed love turned to loathing. Despite her pleas, Amnon spoke harshly to Tamar and ordered a servant to throw her out of the house and bolt the door behind her.

What was Tamar to do? She ripped her long-sleeved robe and put ashes on her head as a sign of mourning. She then went to her brother Absalom, perhaps the only man she could trust to stand up for her. One would expect David to take action on behalf of his daughter, but the king who defeated Goliath and conquered every enemy is now portrayed as too indecisive or weak to discipline his own children.

Absalom (13:23–15:12)

Even as Absalom comforted his violated sister and urged her not to "take it to heart," he took it to his own heart and swore vengeance against Amnon. Absalom did not act in haste, remaining quiet and biding his time for two years. Then, Absalom put a plan into motion. He invited all the king's sons to a celebration associated with the annual sheep shearing on his estate in Baal-hazor, probably about five miles north of Bethel. He ordered his servants to wait until Amnon got drunk, then to strike him dead.

In the ensuing melee, the other royal sons fled for their lives, fearing that Absalom planned to eliminate all rivals for the throne. Indeed, the first news that came to David insisted that all the king's sons were dead. With a large stroke of irony, the narrator describes how the same Jonadab who had helped Amnon plot Tamar's rape now counsels David, assuring him that Amnon alone had fallen victim to Absalom's plot, since he was the one who deserved it.

Following the murder, Absalom fled to his mother's home in Geshur, not knowing when or if he would be able to return to Jerusalem. He apparently assumed, probably correctly, that David might have let Amnon get away with rape, but could not afford to let him get away with murder.

As he stewed in his self-imposed exile, Absalom's growing megalomania led him to desire the throne without waiting for David's death. Apparently, Absalom perceived his father as weak and incompetent, especially in the area of judgment. When he later stationed himself in the gate of the city and "stole the hearts of the people" by accusing David of caring nothing for justice (15:1-6), perhaps David's failure to demand justice for Tamar fueled his fiery rhetoric.

How the murderous Absalom regained his stature is a story in itself (ch. 14). He appears to have remained in touch with David's general Joab, a man who also preferred to settle scores with a sword (cf. 2 Sam 2:27-28; 18:14-15; 20:9-10). Joab was an early supporter of Absalom and sought to facilitate his return.

Joab persuaded a "wise woman" from the city of Tekoa to approach David, claiming to seek safety for her one remaining son, who had killed his brother in a fit of anger. David agreed with her that it was a terrible thing, and that her other son should be allowed to come home and care for her. David even promised to issue a decree that no harm should come to him. The woman then turned the story back on David (not unlike Nathan's ploy in ch. 12), wondering why he refused to allow his own son Absalom to come home.

Thus persuaded, David allowed Absalom to return to Jerusalem, but still refused to see him for another two years. Absalom had pressured Joab to take his case before David, but Joab refused until Absalom set fire to Joab's harvest-ready fields to press the issue. Joab interceded and set up a meeting between father and son, but the reunion described in 14:33 was obviously forced. Even so, it was an important moment for Absalom because it made him appear to be in David's good graces.

The biblical description of Absalom pictures him as the "Fabio" of the ancient world, so good-looking that "in all Israel there was no one to be praised so much for his beauty as Absalom; from the sole of his foot to the crown of his head there was no blemish in him" (14:25). When Absalom got his annual haircut, his shorn locks reputedly weighed 200 shekels, a hefty five pounds (14:26).

Absalom began his play for the throne by obtaining for himself a chariot with horses and hiring fifty men to serve as royal roadies and bodyguards. He made a habit of stationing himself by the city gate, schmoozing with all who entered and intercepting any who had come seeking justice from the king, insisting that they would find no succor in David. "I only I were judge in the land!" he would say. "Then all who had a suit or cause might come to me, and I would give them justice" (15:4). In this way, over a period of time, Absalom played up discontent with David and promoted himself in such a way that the narrator says "so Absalom stole the hearts of the people of Israel" (15:6).

The reader can't help noting that David, in his earlier life, never allowed anyone to steal anything from him. If any taking was to be done, it was David who did the taking. Now, however, the king is portrayed as too weak or distracted to take any action against the obviously treasonous actions of his own son.

Still needing permission to travel outside of Jerusalem, Absalom used the ruse of an unfulfilled vow to gain his father's leave for a trip to David's former capital in Hebron (15:7-8). The law allowed a father to annul vows made by a wife or daughter, but not a son (Num 30:1-16). Once in Hebron, Absalom mustered his supporters and set in motion a coup d'etat that had a good chance of success.

David and Absalom (15:13–19:8)

David was not unaware of Absalom's ambition, and planned a strategic retreat. As his traitorous son approached Jerusalem with his rebel army, David fled the city, taking with him most of his family, though he left behind ten concubines to look after the palace. On the way out of the city, David was met by a series of people, some of whom were helpful. A relative of Saul, however, rained curses, stones, and dust upon David, calling him a murderer and scoundrel. To the amazement of his associates, a contrite David accepted Shimei's condemnation without complaint (16:5-13).

As David traveled eastward from Jerusalem, two of his best advisors remained in the city. The legendary Ahithophel, whose counsel was said to be like an "oracle of God" (16:23), defected willingly to Absalom's cause. David persuaded another advisor named Hushai to remain behind as a double agent, feigning allegiance to Absalom and negating any good advice that Ahithophel might give.

Ahithophel counseled Absalom to demonstrate his regnal status publicly and cut all ties with his father by claiming David's harem as his own. To make sure no one missed the point, Absalom had a canopy erected on top of the palace, where he sexually assaulted all ten concubines who remained behind, doing so "in the sight of all Israel" (16:22). Absalom's act calls to mind Nathan's prediction that Yahweh would give David's wives to another, who would lie with them in the light of the sun (12:11).

Ahithophel then encouraged Absalom to send a squad to capture David while he was weary and exposed on the road, but Hushai countered with an argument that Absalom should wait until he could call up an overwhelming army of new recruits that could easily sweep over David's small force. Absalom followed Hushai's intentionally bad advice, thus giving David an opportunity to arrive safely in Mahanaim and reconnoiter his forces. Ahithophel was so angry when his advice was ignored that he went home and killed himself.

The final battle account is found in 2 Samuel 18. Absalom foolishly led his rebel troops into a battle with David's seasoned veterans on a battlefield of David's choosing, in a dense forest. Absalom's men were easily separated, and David's men, divided into three companies, methodically decimated Absalom's troops. The narrator reports that 20,000 men died, noting with apparent satisfaction that the forest devoured more soldiers than the sword (18:8).

David had begged his troops to be gentle with Absalom, and when the young man found himself caught in a tree (by the *head*, not the hair), the soldier who found him did no harm, but reported his location to Joab. Despite David's warning, Joab did not hesitate to kill the young pretender. Most translations suggest that he thrust three "darts" or "javelins" through Absalom's heart, but the Hebrew word means "sticks." The Hebrew image suggests that Joab took three large sticks and swung them at Absalom's chest until he knocked him from the tree, allowing ten of his attendants to surround and kill the rebel leader.

The story of how the news was brought to David is heart wrenching. The king's army had triumphed over his treacherous son, but Absalom's death broke David's heart, and he mourned for the black sheep of his family so loudly that Joab had to counsel restraint lest his loyal soldiers feel unappreciated (19:1-8).

What can we learn from this extended soap opera, from these *Days of Their Lives?* The story of Absalom's rebellion makes it clear that many in Israel had failed to seek *The Guiding Light* of God's intended plans. In fact, the extended account relates one bad decision after another. The reader will notice that God is almost never mentioned in 2 Samuel 13–19. When David and his sons tried to work things out without regard for the Lord's guidance, their lives descended into darkness and death. Those who have ears to hear, let them hear.

David and Modern Readers

The Deuteronomistic historian tells us stories about David that we do not find elsewhere. If you read the account of David's rise and rule in 1 Chronicles 10–29, for example, the king appears faultless from beginning to end. His sin with Bathsheba and against Uriah is never mentioned, nor are the interfamily conflicts affecting his children. In Chronicles, David grows old but never weak as he supervises the establishment of the temple system and its huge staff, and forcefully installs his son Solomon as his successor. The books we call 1–2 Chronicles were written much later than 1–2 Samuel, during the post-exilic period when the surviving religious leaders promoted renewed faithfulness to the temple as the key to pleasing God, so they emphasized those aspects and activities of David.

The editors of 1–2 Samuel, however, worked during the exilic period, and their main intent was to convince the people of Israel that their sins had brought them low, that their failure to live in obedience to God had brought on the exile as punishment for their sins. Thus, even the great David is shown to be subject to the Deuteronomistic principle that the faithful are blessed while the rebellious are cursed. Once David turned his heart from following God's way and chose to follow his own way, it was all downhill from there. David was forgiven but not absolved from the consequences of his sin.

As followers of Christ, we now understand that there is more to our relationship with God than a tit-for-tat arrangement in which obedience automatically opens the tap from which blessings flow, and vice versa. Even so, the story is a reminder that every act has consequences, and the choices we make today may be felt through the remainder of our days, all the *Days of Our Lives*.

1. Amnon was David's oldest son and could have been the presumptive prince who would follow him on the throne. He was filled with potential, but he squandered it: Amnon proved faithless to his sister, his family, and his God. What opportunities for service lie in you? Are you living up to the potential God has put in you?

_____

_____

_____

_____

2. Tamar suffered greatly as the result of Amnon's actions. Have you ever suffered because of someone else's sin? How did you respond to the sense of pain or loss that you did not deserve?

_____

_____

_____

_____

3. Reflecting on David's earlier sin, which opened the door to so many more, can you think of other situations in which one crime/sin/act of violence leads to another? Does vengeance really make things better?

_____

_____

_____

_____

4. Do you have any personal experiences that might illustrate the question above?

_____

_____

_____

_____

5. How do you think David lost control of his children so completely? Once they were grown, was there anything he could have done to regain a measure of influence in the eyes of his family?

_____

_____

_____

_____

_____

6. After losing control of his family, David also lost control of his kingdom, leaving his concubines unprotected as he left Jerusalem in disgrace. Yet, due mainly to the skills and devotion of his army, Absalom's forces were defeated and David regained the throne. Even so, his influence was diminished. Can you think of contemporary examples in which improper actions have led to public disgrace and compromised someone's ability to lead?

_____

_____

_____

_____

_____

7. Do a quick mental review of this extended narrative. Think about the decisions made by major characters in the story. Where did David, Amnon, and Absalom go wrong? What advice would you have given each of them? Can you see any connections between their actions and decisions that you have faced?

_____

_____

_____

_____

_____